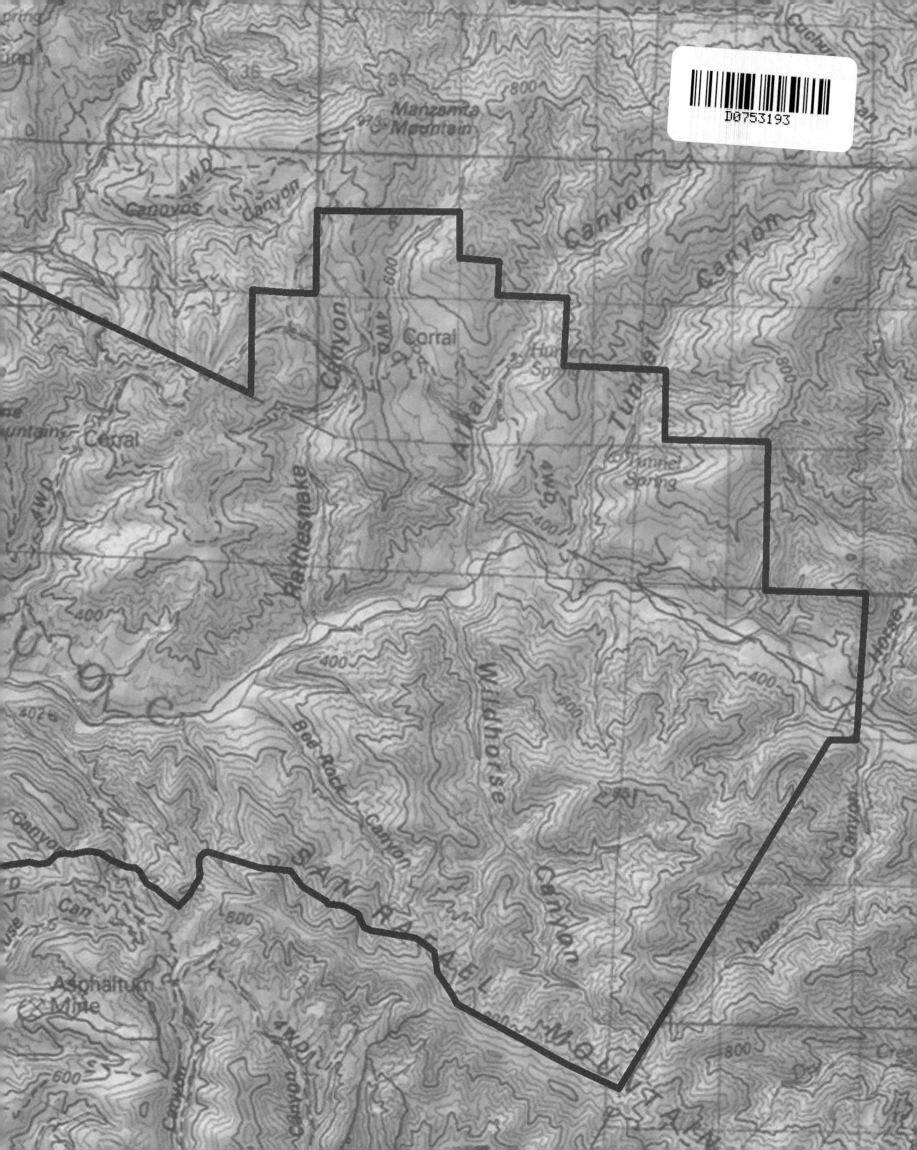

RANCHO SISQUOC

RANCHO SISQUOC

ENDURING LEGACY OF
AN HISTORIC
LAND GRANT RANCH

JUDITH FLOOD WILBUR
CHASE REYNOLDS EWALD

ORO

Contents

FOREWORD by Jerry Brown   9
FOREWORD by Stephen T. Hearst   10
FOREWORD by Eric Hvolboll   13
PROLOGUE by Lisa Flood   14
INTRODUCTION by Judy Flood Wilbur   21

Existing at the Limits   23

Flood, Fire & Drought   33

All Living Things   49

Ranchero: The Land Grant Era   63

The New California   73

Taming the Land   81

Seven Decades of Stewardship   93

Life on Rancho Sisquoc   107

Vineyard View   127

Culture & Community   141

Inspired by the Land   155

RESOURCES
Timeline for Rancho Sisquoc and the Santa Barbara Region   170
Authors and Contributors   173
Land Grant Ranchos of Santa Barbara County   174
Glossary and Place Names   175
Acknowledgments   177

Foreword

California is a state full of wonders and storied places: Silicon Valley, Hollywood, San Francisco, Yosemite, to name only a few. But far from these destinations of renown, other places and other stories play their part in defining the special quality of California. In this wonderful book about the historic Rancho Sisquoc, Judy Flood Wilbur shares her experiences of her family's extraordinary ranch, kept intact—and worked continuously—since before the time when California became a state in 1850.

My family's experience goes back to early California as well, but in the northern part of the state. My father's grandfather, August Schuckman, came across the plains in a wagon train and arrived in Hangtown—now the city of Placerville—in 1852. To escape the often flooded Sacramento River, he made his way to Colusa, then the leading county in the state for producing wheat. He farmed in a number of places and eventually purchased the Mountain House, a stagecoach stop and hotel at the junction of Leesville Road and Wilbur Road, 20 miles west of the Sacramento River. Here the Leesville Ladoga stage stopped each day for fresh horses before continuing farther west to the many spas or mines that then dotted the landscape.

August and his wife, Augusta, had eight children. My grandmother, Ida, was the youngest, born in 1878, a time of pioneers and homesteading in this part of Colusa, which was then vibrant with a dozen young families. But Ida was restless and fiercely independent, so at 18, with two neighbor girls, she set off for San Francisco, where she met and married my grandfather, Edmund Joseph Brown. Many years later, she would be my babysitter and tell me countless stories about life at the Mountain House and the unusual people she would encounter. It was a special place, she told me, and I never forgot that. In the years leading up to World War I, the homesteaders started leaving, the local school closed, and, with the coming of the automobile, the Leesville Stage ceased operating. By the 1930s only tenants remained, and by 1948 even they had departed. Still, the Mountain House kept its magic and served as the gathering place for countless descendants of August and Augusta.

When my father died, I took over his share of what was then a 2,500-acre ranch called Rancho Venada. I knew that one day I would restore the Mountain House and possibly even find a way to live there. My grandmother's words stayed with me and got stronger as the years went on. In 2017, my wife, Anne, and I started construction on Mountain III, (the first was built in 1855, the second in 1907) and took up actual residence the day after I completed my final term as governor of California.

That is where we live today. We restored the old barns, dug new wells, and brought in 110 olive trees, which, when harvested and blended with older trees from the Schuckman era, make excellent Mountain House Olive Oil. The pioneer days are gone, but the land and the hospitality remain. At dawn, the sun comes over the mountains and at night, bright stars and the Milky Way fill the darkened sky. The magic and the memories remain.

—*Jerry Brown*

Foreword

Judy Wilbur asked me to write a little something about my family's experience in California ranching. Seven generations of Hearst Family members have had the privilege of working on and enjoying our San Simeon Ranch. The registered name of the San Simeon property is Rancho Piedra Blanca. This name references the white rocks off the coast of the property—white due to centuries of bird guano. This ranch is 18 miles north to south and 15 miles west to east; 83,000 acres, or 130 square miles. George Hearst, William Randolph Hearst's father, purchased the land in 1865. George was a successful miner and eventually a successful politician.

WR was two years old when George purchased the ranch. The ranch has always been a working ranch raising cattle, horses, hogs, and farming many acres to grow hay, beans, and avocados, among several other crops. But the main attraction is the property. From the Pacific Ocean to east of the Santa Lucia Mountains, these are some of the most beautiful landscapes anywhere in the world. We have enjoyed this place for over 150 years, and still feel like we are just getting started. When you see the seventh generation of young people showing up for vacations and holiday gatherings, it is fantastic to watch how they enjoy the surroundings. And then you realize, years ago, that was us.

I have known several large landowners and ranchers over the years, and it is always enjoyable to hear their stories of growing up on their ranches: learning to ride and rope; being taught how to drive at the age of five or so. Our first vehicle was a 1949 Willys Jeep. Dad would pull out the hand-throttle in low range, step out of the Jeep and walk alongside until we were all set sitting on the boat cushions so we could see through the steering wheel. What greater fun could kids have on a summer day at the ranch. Then there were the rides, the picnics, and the races!

These were wonderful times, and they still are incredible. It's about the family, the vistas, the wildlife, and spending time with cows and horses. Please enjoy this story about the history of Rancho Sisquoc and the people who tell their story. It is about a way of life.

—*Stephen T. Hearst*

Foreword

Rancho Sisquoc is a California anachronism. Several cities could fit within its 58 square miles, with wide ranges of chaparral-covered hills left over. Like a fugitive fleeing from the scourge of urbanization, which has eradicated what once made chimerical California a dream, Rancho Sisquoc seeks and finds refuge in the wilderness.

Rancho Sisquoc watches—for a soaring California condor searching for carrion after making its last wild stand in the Sierra Madre above the ranch, for a heifer's first calf, for the ripening of its rare Sylvaner wine grapes, for the first spring wildflowers and late blooming poppies, for the cowboys' return as the ranch kids clandestinely braid horses' manes and tails, for ticks, poison oak, nettles, rattlesnakes, badgers, trespassers, for dangerous flash floods, and for the future that constantly creeps into the ranch, most recently in the form of the first internet antennas on its northern hills.

Rancho Sisquoc smells—of leather saddles marinated in horse sweat, of diesel tractors maintaining almost 100 miles of dirt roads, of gooey eggs, pinquito beans, and raw bacon baked into the old walls of Mrs. Moreno's cookhouse, of burning steerhide under a hot branding iron, of cow chips, of dogs after a skunk fight, of barbecue and wildfire smoke, of deer jerky drying in the sun outside the slaughterhouse, and, more recently, of its own wine aging in oak barrels.

Rancho Sisquoc listens—to the Sisquoc River rolling over shale rocks, to coyotes yapping at dusk, to woodpeckers and flickers assaulting its oaks, to kids jumping into the Bee Rock swimming hole, to mountain lions' screams, bobcats' snarls, and wild turkeys' gobbles, to wind whipping down the river from Big Pine Mountain, to farmworkers' trucks downshifting as they drive through the riverbed to broccoli and cauliflower fields, to vineyard workers' easy language mixing of Spanish and English, to laughing visitors on the tasting room lawn, to the low mooing of mother cows to their newborn calves at night, and to the whoosh of a gas burner coming to life on Betty Flood's 1921 Quick Meal stove to heat morning coffee.

Rancho Sisquoc echoes—of generations of indigenous people fishing in and walking up the river canyon to the Cuyama and collecting the river's thick-stemmed tules (which were burned so the pith could be sprinkled on a newborn after its umbilical cord was cut for quick healing), of past sugar beet, garbanzo, and hay fields, of droughts, of Mexican mestizo owners and workers and almost forgotten people and happenings memorialized in canyons' place names like Schoolhouse, Round Corral, Wild Horse, Rattlesnake, Alejandro, Bell, and of big men like Vicente Castro, Thomas Bishop, Robert Easton, and James Flood.

Rancho Sisquoc was one of the last Mexican land grants awarded before the American conquest of California commenced in the 1840s. The ranch boundary configuration today remains relatively unchanged and 20th-century land purchases have augmented its original 35,000 acres, easily making it the largest ranch left in Santa Barbara County. San Francisco's Flood family has played a large role in California history ever since the Gold Rush and continues its community service today at Rancho Sisquoc by maintaining this remarkable, expansive ranch unsubdivided.

I am grateful for every opportunity to visit Rancho Sisquoc. When there my favorite mental echo is the sound of Betty Flood's 1956 Land Rover, which she drove for many years over the ranch's rough dirt roads well into her nineties—and well past the time the Land Rover's brakes worked reliably, especially when wet after a river crossing. Betty didn't care; she knew how to drive the five-gear stick shift and to brake by using the clutch. I recall bouncing around the bare metal back of the old Land Rover with Judy Wilbur almost 20 years ago as Betty drove right through the rugged, uneven Sisquoc riverbed without any hesitation or deceleration. I must have appeared anxious, because Judy said to me laughingly, "Don't worry, Eric. Mom's been driving this way for years."

—*Eric Hvolboll*
La Paloma Ranch, Gaviota

Prologue

"Wonderful time."
—Ganno, from the ranch guest book

Most everyone in the Flood family would agree that the best time you can have at Rancho Sisquoc is driving across the ranch in the 1950s Land Rovers, one of which Dad brought directly from Africa. For most of my childhood Grandpa or Grandma drove; later my father took the wheel. Always to the sound of a tooting horn, we clambered into the back of the Rovers, next to straw picnic baskets and a motley crew of dogs. The groan of the gear shift, the clouds of dust promised a day full of adventure and often lunch at Bee Rock, a magnificent swimming hole. My aunt Elizabeth remembers these drives as a child when Grandpa drove, and Uncle Ward, riding shotgun, wore bananas in his ears to make her laugh.

Most of us learned to drive these old manual Rovers from our elders, even before we could touch the pedals. Our teachers hollered as we careened next to cliffs, ground the gears, reversed instead of pulling forward, or stalled in the river. Besides learning to balance the clutch and accelerator, we always had something to do. We checked on the vineyards, the river, the garbanzo beans, or picked oranges for juice the following morning. Sometimes we checked on the cows, picked watercress up LaBrea, or stopped for a dip in the reservoir. Aunt Joan remembers accompanying young Jimmie. He drove; she looked for wildlife. If Grandpa or Dad drove, they told stories nonstop about the place. They pointed out the new grapes, discussed the cattle outfit, and recounted stories about the land we were all lucky to share. One regular guest referred to Dad's epic tours as "Jim Flood's Safaris."

An invitation to the ranch always felt special. One of the most anticipated events of the year was Thanksgiving. Every year, nearly twenty relatives in pilgrim hats sat shoulder to shoulder around the kitchen table covered with a brightly colored oil cloth and decorated with a Lazy Susan crowded with everything from salt and pepper to ketchup and honey. Extra kids perched at the red linoleum counter with a good view of Grandma and Aunt Jean juggling pots and cast-iron skillets on a quirky white 1921 gas stove called a Quick Meal.

"Good turkey."
—Grandpa

"And dressing."
—Russ, a friend

A group of us competed at the Santa Barbara Horse Show at the nearby Earl Warren showgrounds during Thanksgiving. While we loved competing, the equestrian bunch couldn't wait to get back to the ranch to hear about the day at the Sisquoc, a day most likely spent driving the Rovers, riding horses, picnicking, and hunting upland birds. We loved reuniting with our cousins. After a festive dinner, we played charades for hours in a cozy living room decorated with Grandma's needlepoint rug and an old Colt 45 tacked on the wall. Periodically, the phone would ring. One buzz meant the office. Don't answer. Two buzzes meant a friend was calling in to wish us a happy holiday. Pick up!

I loved the holiday flurry of family at Sisquoc, the coming and going of relatives in and out of the ranch house and in and out of the girls' and boys' quarters, announced by the friendly, comforting thunk of screen doors. We always gathered on Grandma's terrace, a welcoming place with bougainvillea and her favorite potted geraniums and a small gate that must remain closed to keep the dogs from escaping. For a week or so we thrived, supported by our large, boisterous family. Hands-down, everyone's favorite Thanksgiving guest was our Uncle Johnny, Dad's younger brother, a cowboy with many tall tales, who had lived on the ranch for a time with his pet otter named Oscar.

"The ranch is lovely. The hospitality better."
—Francis K. Marshall

Of course the fun of the ranch was donning a straw hat and living like a cowboy. We all loved to ride. We had learned to ride early, and we watched our grandmother move cattle well into her eighties. She once told me she never understood trail riding. She preferred to ride with the head cowboy Ron Davis and his crew. They moved the cows out of the brush and did ranch chores like checking on the irrigation or the state of a cow pasture or watering trough. Aunt Joan liked cowboy work too. "Judy and I weren't interested in just riding around and picking daisies," she said. "We wanted to ride with the cowboys and do ranch work." At first this took some convincing, but soon the cowboys realized the family could ride. Throughout the years, most of us participated in cattle drives and brandings. Grandpa used to wake the sleepy kids at 7 am and hustle them over to breakfast in the cookhouse full of cowboys and cigarette smoke. Work and riding under a hot California sun followed.

"Helped Astrid learn how to fall off a horse."
—Richard Colyear

"It's a heck of a training program."
—Astrid Sommer

In celebration of my grandmother's 80th birthday, nearly our entire family spent a western weekend, organized by my Aunt Judy and Aunt Elizabeth at the Tunnell House, a homestead cabin at the end of the ranch. The first day, the family participated in a treasure hunt across the ranch; the following day some people hiked, others rode horses further up the river to more homesteads and the Manzana Schoolhouse. Throughout the weekend, we ate catered meals, played games, and camped out under the magnificent oak trees. Grandma, who had Hollywood looks her whole life, posed for portraits in Grandpa's old woolly chaps and a western shirt. One evening, all the grandchildren, playing the parts of Grandma's past dogs, performed a skit written by our cousin Jennifer. The adult audience, perched on stumps, dressed in serapes and slouchy sombreros, howled with laughter as the sun set on the Los Padres National Forest.

On the way back to ranch headquarters at the end of this birthday weekend, a bunch of us—the Gambles, the Wilburs, the Stevensons, my sisters—filled with the joy and giddiness that comes with being outdoors in the fresh air, looked back once, then galloped full-throttle across the upper mesa—the thunder of hooves the only sound in our ears—like bandits on the silver screen.

Of course, ranch life brought us all close to wildlife. The ranch teemed with quail, doves, deer, wild pigs, turkeys, and the magnificent condors. Mountain lions roamed the hills, preying on the cattle; bears helped themselves to the grapes in the McMurray Vineyard. On Elizabeth's first date on the ranch with her future husband, she hollered at him to stop the Rover and shot a boar for dinner from the passenger window. One summer afternoon, Judy and Joan bravely chopped the head off a rattlesnake moving dangerously near the cook house.

Ranch life didn't suit everyone. My great-grandmother, Maude Lee Flood, who lived in the Fairmont Hotel Penthouse (the Swig Penthouse) on Nob Hill, came to the ranch once. She wore formal city attire with a posh black hat and veil. As the story goes, Grandpa drove her to an oak tree grove just past the Dam Corral. She told him the oak trees were beautiful, then returned to the city and never came back.

"A perfect day."
—Maude Lee Flood

After Grandpa died in 1990, my father, an executive vice president at Wells Fargo Bank at the time, took the reins as president of the ranch. He worked closely with Mary and Ed Holt, who raised their family on the Sisquoc and managed the ranch for 35 years. Following in Grandpa's footsteps, Dad was a hands-on guy, the Holts both said. He talked to everyone and wanted to know if they liked their job and were being treated well. He worked relentlessly with the Holts to make the ranch finally financially sustainable. He found a home sitting around the Holts' kitchen table, sharing wine, and laughs and talking about the Sisquoc.

"He would always dig into whatever was happening on the ranch," Mary Holt said. "He loved the branding. He loved to get on horseback and be a cowboy."

"Built a road."
—Grandpa

"Planned a new irrigation system."
—Uncle Ward

"Planted the Sauvignon Blanc."
—Dad

Dad was also passionate about developing the winery. Under his watch, the winery grew from a few hundred cases to 20,000. The ranch winemaker Sarah Holt, Ed and Mary's daughter, also succeeded in achieving one of Dad's dreams: a high score of 91 points and Editor's Choice in Wine Enthusiast Magazine for Rancho Sisquoc's 2019 Sauvignon Blanc.

My father also enjoyed hosting, along with his sister Judy and their mother, the annual wine club party, where he captivated his audience with good humor, his signature cackle, and brilliant storytelling. And with his daughter Karin, they sipped wine, enjoyed a traditional Santa Maria barbecue, and challenged their guests to Cow Plop Bingo.

"A long way from chaos."
—Dick Elkus

When Grandma agreed to have my wedding at the ranch, she set in motion preparations for one of the most spectacular gatherings of family and friends at the ranch that I have ever known. My husband, Thomas, and I said, "I do" in the San Ramon Chapel with our dog Moose by our side. We received people from all over the country at the winery, then rode in a wooden wagon pulled by a draft horse team down a lane my father lit with round paper lanterns to a spectacular reception in the bull barn. Guests from San Francisco and Wyoming sipped vichychoisse soup and two-stepped to western ditties performed by Hot Club of Cowtown as the bulls looked on from either side of the open barn.

"We had a marvelous time."
—Grandma

When the last guests left with jars of ranch honey tucked under their arms, Dad looked at me, my husband, sister, and some friends and said, "Anybody want to go on a bear hunt?" Rumor had it that a bear was up enjoying the Sauvignon Blanc grapes and Dad wanted to see him.

We spent the next hour roaring around the ranch under the moonlight. Finally with no luck, Dad deposited Thomas and me at a wall tent in the vineyards where we would spend our wedding night. But not without another champagne toast. Candlelight illuminated a canvas room with a bed up on hay bales, a rattan rocker, and a Victrola. Mom, who had designed the whole space, left instructions for the music. First, we popped the champagne. Then we cranked the record player as far as it would go and lay the needle down on an old 78. A tune called "The Girl That I Marry," from the 1946 musical *Annie Get Your Gun,* crackled into the air. We cried and hugged and laughed, making rowdy noises I'm sure the Sauvignon Blanc bear could hear.

More recently my husband, our two young children, and I sat with my grandmother on the sandy Sisquoc riverbed and admired a newly uncovered whale skeleton. We spoke about the marvel of Sisquoc once being covered by the sea and probably about our shared love of Italy and Dean Martin and horses, of course. Possibly she told stories about her travels around the world and entertaining presidents and diplomats as my kids balanced on rocks and searched for fossils in the fresh spring air.

Rancho Sisquoc is a family place where generations have played together and will continue to do so. Even when apart from Sisquoc, I carry the place in my heart and imagination. Something about the ranch has somehow shaped us all. There must have been something in the dirt.

In 2020, I watched my father thoughtfully cinch his silver cowboy buckle, the one he wore every day with business suits, ski suits, and Levis, for the last time. For his whole life, the cowboy persona defined him as it has defined all of us. Over the years Rancho Sisquoc nourished all of us with a grounding feeling one gets from connection to family and to a place. I'm grateful for this country's generosity.

—*Lisa Flood*

Introduction

After my father purchased Rancho Sisquoc in 1952, I was taken to the ranch for the first time at age eleven. Riding with the cowboys was one of my favorite memories. Mrs. Morrell who ran the cookhouse would prepare, at 6:30 every morning, hardy, greasy fried eggs with potatoes for the cowboys who lived in the bunkhouse. After breakfast, we would often accompany them to gather cattle from LaBrea or Sisquoc or work the cattle in the corrals. The biggest adventure was riding ten miles up to the Tunnell House where we would camp and then spend the next several days rounding up cattle from rough terrain up Rattlesnake, Alkali, and the Manzana Schoolhouse canyon area.

Another highlight as a teenager was learning to drive the 1956 five-gear, four-wheel-drive Land Rover. Our family often spent summers and holidays on the ranch, and as I grew up, I visited on and off for many years, which I am still doing today.

For the 25th anniversary of Rancho Sisquoc Winery, I created a book for the family describing the many aspects of the ranch. In 2022, with the ranch celebrating 70 years of family ownership and 50 years of Rancho Sisquoc wines, it seemed appropriate to publish an expanded version to share this enduring legacy of the historic Rancho Sisquoc.

Rancho Sisquoc played an important role in early California history, and still does in modern times. It is one of the few remaining intact land grants given by the last Governor of Mexico, Señor Pío Pico, in the mid-1800s and consists of some 37,000 acres. A first-time visitor arriving at the front gate is overwhelmed by the dramatic view up the valley to the rugged mountain ranges in the far distance. The early morning fog, which rolls in quietly during the night, gives way just before noon to sparkling sunshine. This magical land is awe-inspiring in so many ways. As a working ranch with expansive vegetable fields, and cattle grazing in the pastures at the headquarters, and nearby vineyards on large mesas going up the Sisquoc River toward the east, it provides a dramatic contrast between the cultivated land and the wildness of the backcountry where one finds a stillness and oneness with nature.

The Sisquoc River, which is at the heart of the property, is a major force. From its flooding at times to being nearly bone dry at others, the river provides a home to many and varied wildlife, fauna, flora, rock formations, and fossils.

Additionally, there are so many colorful stories of the people who lived there long ago and of more recent inhabitants, which make it impossible to capture them all. I have tried to recount some of these characters and their stories in this book.

It is my hope that this enduring legacy of our working ranch will live on for many generations, and that our tradition of thoughtful stewardship will continue to preserve and respect the land.

—Judy Flood Wilbur

Existing at the Limits

Rancho Sisquoc is defined by the Sisquoc River, which bisects it diagonally for about fifteen miles, provides its water, and acts as its organizing force. The river originates in the San Rafael Mountains, flowing from a massive wilderness system of approximately 1.75 million acres now known as the Los Padres National Forest. The forest system encompasses a range of ecosystems including redwood forests, mixed conifer forests, oak woodlands, grasslands, pinyon juniper stands, chaparral, and semi-desert areas. These provide habitat for more than 468 fish and wildlife species including bears, mountain lions, and the California Condor.

Originating at 6,320 feet on the northern slopes of Big Pine Mountain, Sisquoc's headwaters are located above Sisquoc Falls, in the most impenetrable part of the forest. It is such rough country that 19th-century backcountry guides advised taking along "a sheet-iron suit of clothes."

The first half of the river flows through the Los Padres National Forest, part of which is now the San Rafael Wilderness; designated in 1968, it became the first primitive area in the nation classified as wilderness under the Wilderness Act of 1964. In 1992 this was expanded with the creation of the Los Padres Condor Range and the passage of the River Protection Act, when a thirty-three-mile stretch of the river, from its headwaters to the national forest border, was designated "wild and scenic" as part of the National Wild

and Scenic Rivers system. The Sisquoc runs for more than fifty-seven miles and drains much of Santa Barbara County. It joins the Cuyama River twenty miles upstream from the Pacific Ocean at the border of Santa Barbara County and San Luis Obispo County, where it becomes the Santa Maria River. During the Miocene Epoch, most of California's Central Coast, including the Sisquoc Valley, was below sea level. Following eons of geological events — ice ages, volcanic activity, earthquakes, and erosion — the California coast was lifted above sea level, leaving behind limestone formations, fossils, tar deposits and mesas throughout the valley.

The rocks exposed on Rancho Sisquoc record a long history of tectonic upheaval and drastic environmental changes along the California coast over 100 million years, according

to Dr. Nate Onderdonk, professor of Geological Sciences at California State University, Long Beach. Almost all the rocks on the ranch are sedimentary, formed by the hardening of sand, silt, and clay particles that settled on the bottom of an ocean. The oldest of these formed during the Cretaceous Period, when this part of California was a subduction zone where an oceanic plate on the west was diving beneath the North American continent. This subduction zone created the Sierra Nevada mountains, while the ancient rivers that cut into these mountains brought sediment down to the coastal waters along the edge of the continent, where it was deposited and later hardened into rock. Cretaceous sedimentary rocks are now found in the eastern parts of the ranch in the deep canyons that cut into the San Rafael Mountains.

Millions of years later, as the movement of the plates changed and the San Andreas fault began to form, huge chunks of crust were ripped apart and small but deep ocean basins were formed along the California coast. Sediment deposited

in these basins later hardened and became the light-colored shale rocks that underlie most of Rancho Sisquoc. These sedimentary rocks include the Sisquoc Formation, named for the Sisquoc River where the formation was first studied. These rocks contained plentiful plant and animal debris, which was transformed into oil as the rocks were buried and heated. Today, tar and oil visibly seep from the rocks in some places, and there are numerous oil fields around the ranch that have been active for almost a century. As the San Andreas fault system continued to develop, tectonic squeezing lifted the rocks to form the mountains and hills that now make up the dramatic scenery along the Sisquoc River. The river has been cutting down through the mountains as they rise, forming wide terraces that now provide ideal locations for the vineyards that have been planted along the river. Many of these mesas have proved very productive; the Big Mesa, the Little Mesa, the Bryant, and the McMurray have been farmed for decades.

The Sisquoc River flows from the high elevations of the Los Padres National Forest and bisects Rancho Sisquoc for approximately fifteen miles. The sedimentary rocks that define the region include tar and oil deposits. Although various oil companies explored the ranch, the oil has been deemed unsuitable for commercial use. In 1986, a pipeline was installed to transport oil from the Santa Barbara area across the ranch to refineries in Bakersfield and Nopomo.

Fossils can be found throughout ranch property and attest to an earlier era when the land was covered by sea. Ron Davis once found a whale vertebrae on Bone Mountain while gathering cattle. Two other whale skeletons were found in the Sisquoc River.

In places, evidence of this geologic activity is visible even to the untrained eye. In his online blog *Jack Elliott's Santa Barbara Adventures*, the author cites an 1884 narrative published in the *Santa Maria Times*. In the account, two leaders from the community of homesteaders located upstream from Rancho Sisquoc guided a group to the uncharted territory above the main waterfall on the river, which they measured at 480 feet in height. "Near the top of the bluff, and at an elevation of 4,000 feet above sea, is an old beach line about fifty feet thick of rocks and marine shells deeply cemented together. This is the fifth well defined beach line to be found at the various altitudes between this place and the summit at the San Rafael range, all of them showing a different age and different formation of rocks. We found marine shells, etc., in the sandstone at the extreme summit of the range, at an altitude of over 5,000 feet."

Cattle manager Ron Davis found a whale vertebrae on Bone Mountain and two whale skeletons were discovered in the Sisquoc River below the LaBrea crossing. One of these was found by Matt Holt, son of then managers Ed and Mary Holt. That skeleton is now housed at the Natural History Museum of Los Angeles County. Fossils are plentiful on the ranch and have been unearthed behind the Horse Barn, below the Oak Tree Mesa, and in many other locations throughout the ranch.

The indigenous people of the area, the Chumash, depended largely on deer and other game, fish, yucca, pine nuts from the foothill pines, and live oak acorns, which they made into mash.

The people who originally inhabited this region were natives of the Chumash tribe who called the upper end of the Santa Maria Valley "Sisquoc." Their range extended from the Channel Islands to the coastal mountains and from Morro Bay to Malibu. The mild climate and plentiful resources of the region made it possible for the Chumash to live as hunter-gatherers in small bands. They had both permanent villages and intermittent camps, with interior mainland Chumash depending largely on deer, fish, yucca, pine nuts and live oak acorns, which were made into a mash. The arrival of the Spanish in 1770 was pivotal, and devastating, for the region's natives as it led to the establishment of the missions, meant to westernize the indigenous people but ultimately creating a serf-like system. The arrival of home-steaders, soldiers and ranchers took a further toll as tradi-tional Chumash lands became settled. Researchers believe that there weren't any Chumash villages on Rancho Sisquoc, but that an encampment existed further upstream near the homesteaders' lands on the Manzana. Evidence of their passing through Sisquoc lands exists today in the form of well-worn pounding stones and other remnants.

Joan Easton Lentz, an ornithologist whose grandfather ran Rancho Sisquoc and whose father was raised there, has made some trips deep into the wilderness near the Sisquoc River's headwaters. In June 1999 she wrote, "After dinner we watch the sunset. If you stand and face north you see the ranges of the Sierra Madre, Caliente and Temblor mountains in purple links of color fast disappearing in the mist of the evening. And to the west — down the Sisquoc — more folded ridges as the flanks of the San Rafael dip down all the way toward the Sisquoc Ranch and Santa Maria… I love the parade — the high mountain forest of green pines and firs juxtaposed with the yucca-studded slopes at lower elevations… These southern ranges aren't glamorous mountains. They have no snow-capped peaks, rushing streams, spires or deep lakes. What they do have is a spare quality of land existing at its limits."

Existing at the Limits

Flood, Fire & Drought

Children growing up on Sisquoc Ranch, if not helping move cattle or doing other chores, were allowed, even expected, to spend the day outside: on a horse, by the river, or exploring on their own. It was generally understood that kids were to amuse themselves until dinnertime and not get in the way. While they were warned about hazards such as rattlesnakes and bobcats, they were expected to use common sense, and to learn from experience. The perils of water, however, specifically floods, were something they were warned about in graphic terms. "These 3,000-foot mountains are covered with snow in the winter and when it melts," recalls Judy Flood Wilbur, "flash floods could come down like a wall, out of nowhere."

Floods, like fire and drought, are part of the natural cycle of the seasons. They're an aspect of life that makes ranching in California, despite the temperate climate, one that requires generous helpings of tenacity and faith. But it was the early homesteaders and ranchers of California who had to endure what was arguably the toughest spell in recorded history.

"The winter of 1861–1862 was one of the wettest seasons ever recorded. Floods destroyed large amounts of property of the ranchers, houses of adobe melted down to mud, trails were washed out, roads were obliterated and streams became raging torrents washing away cattle or causing them to become mired down in the mud and quicksand deposited over the lower areas of the land," write E. R. (Jim) Blakley and Karen Barnette in the *Historical Overview Los Padres National Forest.* "The season of the great flood was followed by a great drought, the worst in recorded history in the state of California. No rain fell all year in 1862. There were no winter rains in 1863. There were nothing but sprinkles until late 1864."

Bjorn Rye further describes this hardship in *Ranchos; Santa Barbara Land Grant Ranches*: "Torrential rains fell in November 1861, followed by a storm that began on December 24th and lasted one solid month. The ranches sustained major losses in ruined adobes, orchards, vineyards, fields and drowned stock. Then, following the floods, came the great drought of 1862–64, in which an estimated three million cattle died in southern California. By the spring of 1863 the starving, bawling cattle were desperate for forage. Month after month conditions continued to worsen. Grizzlies, coyotes and cougars feasted on the herds, but by autumn there were more carcasses than they could eat. The land was littered with the dried husks of cattle who had simply stopped in their tracks and fell there. Sundowners whipped the scorched dust into the skies," he continues, "and for months on end the sun was no more than a coppery glow in the yellow haze. In the midst of the drought great clouds of *chapules* — grasshoppers— descended on the land, stripping every last shred of foliage from the parched hillsides."

Despite this near Biblical level of punishment, still no rains came. The drought continued until ranchers resorted to chopping down live oaks as forage and cattle were auctioned in Santa Barbara for less than 38 cents per head. By the time the rains resumed, the number of cattle in Santa Barbara County had plummeted, from 300,000 head to 5,000.

As Rye so poignantly describes, "Heaps of bones lying bleaching in the sun marked an end to the county's ranching economy, an end to the great baronial estates of the unfenced ranchos, and, in time, and end to the grace and hospitality which had characterized the days of *dolce far niente*."

Ranches of course held on. They adapted, and in many cases diversified, as Rancho Sisquoc has. And they will continue to endure, despite ever more challenging conditions created by climate change. In some ways, though, the more things change, the more they stay the same. In recalling their years on or near the ranch, Judy Flood Wilbur and Ellen Easton agreed: "Homesteader accounts were the same as today: it was floods and fires. The California cycle has not really changed. One of the [Sisquoc area] homesteaders kept 3,000 sheep to clear the underbrush out. It turns out we should all have been doing this, like the Indians in Yosemite used to do major controlled burns to clear brush and promote grasses."

Drought is a farmer's or rancher's nightmare, but rain can be equally problematic. When it does rain in the winter months, the river can become impassable, and a destructive force. In her history of Rancho Sisquoc, Judy writes, "Dave Sprague, who had formerly cared for wild animals at San Simeon, was riding up the river one day when there was a flash flood. He said he would never have made it back were it not for the fact that he had a 'particularly good swimmin' saddle horse.'"

The flood of 1969 destroyed the permanent pasture and fencing from the Pole Barn down to the cattle manager's house. As then manager Harold Pfeiffer wrote in his ranch recollections, "Big flood of February and March 1969 covered part of the orchard. Sammy marooned for about two weeks. Jim Hall of PG&E offered to get him out by helicopter but Sammy would not leave saying all he needed was cigarettes and dog food."

In 1978, heavy rains and flooding caused significant loss of farmland. Five years later, in 1983, extensive flooding resulted in the loss of more than a hundred acres of valuable farmland; it also caused mudslides behind the ranch headquarters and left large rocks strewn around the manager's house. During that big spring flood, Ed Holt tried to cross the LaBrea in his truck. The vehicle was swept into the current and filled with water as high as the steering wheel. Luckily the CB radio still worked and Ed was able to radio for help. Ranch manager Harold Pfeiffer borrowed a tractor from Rowan Vineyard and managed to get a chain out to Ed, who attached the chain to the truck then dragged himself along the chain through the raging torrent. The truck had to be left overnight until the river subsided; in the morning it was still there — and by some miracle still functioning. Another flood of 1997 also resulted in loss of farmland at the Orange Grove and Tejano Flat. Following the damage in 1983, flooding was mitigated through the digging of a pilot channel below the junction of the river and LaBrea and construction of a revetment fence along the river's edge. The topsoil left over from the operation was later used to reclaim approximately 100 acres of the Gate Field that had been lost — the same acres the Adam Brothers are farming today.

In the 1980s, a new road north of the river below the Big Mesa was engineered by ranch owners James Flood and Jim Flood, ranch manager Ed Holt, and neighbor Steve Will, head of the rock plant divisions at Coast Rock. This has granted year-round access to Sisquoc's lands on the north side of the valley, which in turn has enabled vegetable fields, leased to Adam Brothers, and vineyard acreage on the Big Mesa, leased to Copper Cane, to be farmed throughout the year.

In the early 1980s, Coast Rock (now CalPortland) started mining rock and gravel from the Sisquoc riverbed below the LaBrea/Sisquoc River junction. Active gravel mining ceased in 2000 and today a couple hundred acres of land are being

reclaimed for future agricultural use. In all these projects, ranch owner James Flood, his son Jim Flood, and their ranch managers worked closely with Steve Will, and, more recently, his nephew Kevin Will, in a thriving working relationship that has lasted through a series of corporate entities (Coast Rock, Union Asphalt, and CalPortland).

The Floods have found that lasting partnerships forged with neighbors who have shared interests (Kevin Will actually cowboyed at Rancho Sisquoc for a couple of years), coupled with a long-term outlook, are crucial in dealing with the vagaries of nature.

"For as long as I can remember," Judy says, "you'd have the drought, then the heat, then a huge rain which would change the course of the river. When you read the histories, it's 'the water level is up, the water level is down'. A couple of years ago it was the same thing: first the floods, then sand so thick you could hardly get anywhere. The sand was the result of the fires. After the fire the land is barren; then it rains and you

have a flash flood. For about a year you couldn't get up the LeBrea because of the sand. In some ways", she adds, "nothing has changed."

Rancho Sisquoc is bisected by a river and crisscrossed with springs and intermittent streams; it has a large reservoir and many wells. But when Cattle Manager Ron Davis is asked about hazards for the livestock, he gives a one-word reply: "Drought." The problem, he explains, "happens when it just doesn't rain when you need it. You can be in good shape in January and by March you're in trouble."

The longest drought in recent history lasted from 1984 to 1991. To counter this recurring issue, the ranch relies on springs, windmills (gradually replaced by solar pumps) and human-made reservoirs for catching and storing rainfall. Due to recurring seasons of lower-than-normal precipitation, several heavy duty irrigation pumps draw water from various wells varying from 60 to 500 feet deep.

Inextricably linked to worries about drought is fire. Wildfires

Floods and fires have been frequent occurrences throughout time. After severe flooding in 1983, a revetment fence of several miles was built to protect from flood damage. Steve Will worked with James Flood to accomplish this monumental task. In 1952, the Dalton Fire, started by a faulty PG&E pole, burned close enough to headquarters to threaten ranch property. In 1966 a poacher flying in illegally to hunt attempted to land on Wellman Place; the plane crashed, sparking a fire that consumed 90,000 acres.

have always been part of the circle of life, but in recent years wildfire season has been starting earlier and earlier in a cycle driven partly by climate change and drought conditions, and partly by an accumulation of dry fuel in the forests, growing populations encroaching into the wildlands, and expanding and aging power line networks. In southern California these conditions are exacerbated by the strong, dry Santa Ana winds. It's important, however, to see fire phenomena in a historical perspective. Prior to 1850, it is estimated that approximately four and a half million acres burned every year in California, with thirty-year peaks of activity. This is partly the result of the native peoples' use of controlled burns and the fact that they allowed fires to burn. While fires lasted longer, the more organic approach prevented the build-up of fuel that has caused such devastation in recent years.

In 1952 the Dalton Fire was started by a faulty PG&E power pole. The fire burned from the Cuyama Canyon to Tepusquet then onto the hills facing Sisquoc's ranch headquarters. The ranch was threatened, but the fire was brought under control before encroaching on ranch property. In 1966 a private plane crashed on the Wellman Place, seventeen miles up the Sisquoc River. The resulting conflagration consumed 90,000 acres before being extinguished by firefighters who were brought in from all over the state and spent a week camping on the flat by Montgomery Place.

The single largest fire of California's 2007 wildfire season started on private property by sparks from a grinding machine that was being used to repair a water pipe. The Zaca Fire ultimately burned more than 240,000 acres, 75,000 of which were in the Sisquoc Watershed. "For most of July, the fire had moved to the south, but in early August a flank of the fire crossed the Sisquoc River, a wild and scenic river that is the major drainage in the San Rafael Wilderness," writes Josh McDaniel in *The Zaca Fire: Bridging Fire Science and Management*. "This was a major turning point in the management of the fire as it entered new terrain and a new dense

fuel environment." The Zaca Fire was contained September 4, 2007 and brought under control by October 29, 2007, but not before achieving the designation as the second largest fire in recorded history.

Just two years later, a cooking fire in the San Rafael Wilderness in the Los Padres National Forest caused the LaBrea fire. The campsite was not that of a couple of back-country hikers but run by an illegal marijuana growing operation, believed to be part of a Mexican national drug organization, with an estimated 30,000 marijuana plants worth $90 million. Sparked in August 2009, the fire burned 90,000 acres over two weeks. Controlled burns, also called prescribed burns or hazard reduction burning, have taken place on and near the ranch, part of an extensive project involving the U.S. Forest Service, the U.S. Government, and local ranchers. The job of the latter was to bulldoze fire breaks as close to the burns as possible (a dangerous job that relied on at least a bit of luck), and to provide food and water to the firefighters.

With the summers in the American West becoming ever hotter and dryer, managing fire and water resources will become an increasingly urgent necessity.

All Living Things

California's state flag owes its distinctive design to the grizzly bear, thanks to its once ubiquitous presence across the state. But grizzlies haven't been seen in California since they were hunted and trapped to extinction in the 1920s. Black bears, however, have thrived on Rancho Sisquoc. Today, as in decades past, they are spotted frequently. The resident bears seem to favor the fruits of the vineyards, especially the Merlot grapes found in the Flood Vineyard. When one was found dead at the base of a cliff at that vineyard he was rumored to have fallen while inebriated. On another occasion the ranch Jeep was approaching the vineyard only to find a bear sleeping in the road blocking their path. The bear showed so little interest in the intruders it was assumed he was "sleeping it off."

Bobcats are often seen around the ranch headquarters, stalking past the ranch house at twilight, or perched in a tree next to a meadow. They thrive on rodents in the fields as well as abundant rabbits and small birds. Deer, coyote, fox, skunk, wild pigs, badgers, and rattlesnakes are common sights. Beavers ply the waterways, opossums explore at night, and tarantulas and Black Widow spiders prompt the timid to check their boots before pulling them on. Mountain lions also live on the ranch; they are rarely seen but from time to time their tracks appear in the mud along a creek or in the dust of a trail.

Fish were plentiful prior to the construction of the Twitchell Dam by the Bureau of Reclamation northwest of the ranch in the 1950s. "The Sisquoc River and its tributaries…once supported the second-largest steelhead run in Santa Barbara County," according to Los Padres Forest Watch, November 10, 2010. "Early pioneers as far back as 1879 reported hundreds of steelhead in pools, so numerous that one could catch trout with their bare hands. A historic cabin along the Sisquoc River [Tunnell House] contains charcoal sketches of large fish, along with the dates and names of the anglers who caught them, some measuring more than 24 inches long." Today the children enjoy bass and catfish fishing in the reservoir.

Avian life is diverse, from roadrunners to large flocks of ungainly turkeys. They traverse the lawns at ranch headquarters in stately parade at day's end, then roost in the sycamores along the open river bottom below the McMurray Vineyard. Families of quail, for which the ranch is named, are seen throughout the length of the Sisquoc River drainage, scurrying across the road near the olive-tree-lined entrance and flying up from the chaparral in the wild areas upriver. Golden and bald eagles, doves, pigeons, peregrine falcons, waterfowl, various types of hawks and owls, and untold numbers of songbirds keep the skies busy and the vegetation alive with song.

Of all the birds, it is the condor which holds the most significant place in ranch history. With wings stretching almost ten feet from wing tip to wing tip, the California condor is the largest flying bird in North America. It has black plumage and a bald neck and head with skin in yellow and red patches. It is fierce, strong, and tough. Sacred to some Native Americans and a character in the mythology of others (the Chumash believed the condor was once a white bird who flew too close to fire), the birds can glide on air currents as high as 15,000 feet.

Condors came under threat fairly early during the homesteading days; in the 1930s, longtime Rancho Sisquoc manager Robert E. Easton stepped in to save them. As his granddaughter Joan Easton Lentz writes in her book *Story of a Santa Barbara Birder*, "When [he] learned that a road was contemplated to run from Manzana Creek…up and over Hurricane Deck and along the Sisquoc River, he was determined to stop it. Already he was concerned about the California Condor. He saw the depredations of egg collectors on the condor population, and he believed that this rare species needed to be protected."

The National Audubon Society was ready to put their influence behind the effort but needed to know how many condors lived in the region. Easton and his son, 19-year-old Robert O. Easton, along with neighboring rancher Eugene Johnston and his son Lamar, set out to attract them to Montgomery Portrero so they could get a count. They built a blind, set bait and a couple of days later brought a group to witness the result. Joan Easton describes "a circling mass of ravens, turkey vultures, and the large forms of condors among them. The bait had worked. And the news of the California Condor sighting spread through the ornithological world."

The Sisquoc Condor Sanctuary, the first of its kind, was

established in 1937 and the U.S. Forest Service scrapped its plans to build the road. The sanctuary encompasses more than 1,000 rugged acres near the headwaters of the Sisquoc River, deep within what would become the San Rafael Wilderness. Nevertheless, by 1987 the birds had been driven to extinction in the wild through poaching, lead poisoning, power line accidents, and loss of habitat. The condor has since been successfully bred in captivity and has been reintroduced to the wild in Arizona, Utah, Mexico's Baja California, and in the coastal mountains of central and southern California. And the first condor chick born in captivity — at the San Diego Zoo in 1983, when there were only 22 left alive— was named Sisquoc.

Wildflowers are plentiful on the ranch in the spring, with purple-blue lupine and bright orange California poppies some of the most abundant, as well as flowering yucca and other desert varieties. Betty Flood used to regularly gather watercress from the creek edges and seeps. Every few years, however, after an unusually wet rainy season, conditions will align through the course of fall, winter, and spring for a rare botanical phenomenon called a superbloom. These events generally occur every decade or so in California, but extended drought has taken its toll in recent years. The last significant such phenomena in the region were in 2017 and 2019. That was the year influencers throughout the state were posting photos of themselves among the wildflowers, prompting their followers to head out in subsequent days. Those people then posted, prompting *their* friends to follow suit. For a couple of weeks Californian residents couldn't miss the headlines describing crushing crowds at generally untrammeled locations. But the sight is one to behold, and happens occasionally on Rancho Sisquoc with blooms of California poppies and lupine, among other flowers. When the stars align and lupine and poppies create a swathe of color on Rancho Sisquoc, it is a compelling reason to pause one's work for a moment and marvel at nature's display.

Ranchero: Land Grant Era

On April 17, 1845, Governor Pío Pico, the last Mexican governor of California — who was of African, Native American, and Spanish ancestry, and experienced being the wealthiest cattleman in California to living in near poverty in his final years — approved a grant for the Rancho Sisquoc. The grant consisted of 35,485 acres (eight square leagues) in the form of a rectangle 10.5 miles long and 5.5 miles wide, essentially the entire Sisquoc River drainage for fifteen miles.

Rancho Sisquoc was granted to Maria Antonia Domínguez y Caballero, a member of the distinguished Domínguez family of the Los Angeles area and one of the few women ever to be the recipient of such a grant. Maria's grandfather had arrived in California with the Rivera Expedition of 1781 and was ultimately stationed at the Presidio of Santa Barbara. Maria's father, Joe Antonio Domínguez, had been the recipient of the 1842 land grant of Rancho San Emidio, situated along El Camino Viejo on the eastern edge of the San Joaquin Valley. The Caballero family did not hold onto the ranch for long, however, selling in 1851 to James Huie for $12,500. By 1877 Rockwell Stone owned the ranch; his daughter and son inherited. The son's portion was acquired by William Harris and in 1892 John T. Porter, a Watsonville banker, and Thomas B. Bishop, a San Francisco attorney, acquired the daughter's portion. In 1893, they purchased the Harris portion, becoming sole owners of Rancho Sisquoc.

California's land grant period spanned Spanish and Mexican rule, from 1769 to 1846. (This was approximately the same period during which California's twenty-one missions were active; these had been built by the Spanish Government to gain a toehold in North America and to convert native people to Christianity.) During that time about 300 grants were authorized, most of them about 14 square miles in size. Spanish grants had been set up to revert to the Spanish crown upon the death of the grantee. But because Mexican grants, which began when Mexico achieved independence from Spain in 1821, were designed to encourage settlement, the rancho owners' rights to the lands were granted as permanent and unencumbered. When in 1848 California became a territory of the United States, the rights of Mexican land grant recipients were guaranteed by the Treaty of Guadalupe.

The Mexican-American War started May 13, 1846, with a declaration of war by the United States; the action in California began June 15, 1846 with the Bear Flag Rebellion. Americans took possession of the capital of California at Monterey on July 7, 1846, and armed resistance ended with the signing of the Treaty of Cahuenga on January 13, 1847. Rancho Sisquoc was enough off the beaten track to remain removed from the events of the day. A local historical monument, however, enshrines the story that a nearby neighbor, Benjamin Foxen, the English-born owner of Rancho Tinaquaic, was responsible for convincing John C. Fremont to bypass the area in 1846 on his march south to take Santa Barbara for the United States. Foxen, the marker explains, believed the authorities in Santa Barbara were planning to ambush Fremont's force on the narrow approach to Gaviota Pass; he urged Fremont to instead travel via the Santa Ynez Valley and secure San Marcos Pass before approaching the town. Historians differ as to whether Fremont had already decided to take that route, but he did meet with Foxen to acquire horses and local knowledge; Fremont no doubt would have received advice on his options for approaching Santa Barbara, and Foxen, reportedly, served as a guide to San Marcos Pass. The campaign, of course, was successful. Fremont took Santa Barbara without bloodshed and Foxen was later harassed by some Mexican loyalists for aiding the Americans. Foxen is buried in the cemetery of the San Ramon Chapel on a small bluff above the entrance to Rancho Sisquoc.

Rancho Sisquoc was granted to María Antonia Domínguez y Caballero in 1845 by Pío Pico, the last Mexican governor of California. At one time one of the richest men in California, Pico, like many Californios, had a passion for gambling (in particular, the card game Monte) but little cash to gamble with, only land and livestock. As a result, Pico died in poverty. Early settlers in the Santa Maria Valley included Benjamin Foxen, who in 1846 offered John C. Fremont navigational advice which helped him take Santa Barbara from Mexico without bloodshed. The San Ramon Chapel, which perches above the Rancho Sisquoc's entrance gate, was built by the early settlers in memory of Foxen. Many descendants of the original families still live in the Santa Maria Valley.

The land grant period — or era of the great rancheros — has been romanticized, but it was indeed a gracious life with vast lands, ample grass, plentiful wildlife, a pleasant climate, a small population, and a high degree of isolation. Life on the ranchos revolved around family (people tended to intermarry with other families and native people in the region), church, animals, and the land. Tradition, courtesy, and hospitality were emphasized, hierarchical structures maintained, and in this "new world," appearance was of paramount importance.

Equestrian skill was equally prized in a land where horses reflected a person's status and wealth. In *Horses & Horsemanship from the Ranchos of California,* Robert G. Cowan writes, "The ranchero invariably kept a horse saddled before his door, awaiting his pleasure. If it was necessary to go more than fifty steps, he rode. …There were few in the world who could surpass the rancheros and his vaquero in horsemanship. At the age of four or five the boys were placed in the saddle, and either became very expert riders or were killed in the trying. The girls also rode. In fact, there were few who could not ride well. It was customary to ride at a fast gallop until the horse tired. There was no intermediate speed used."

Richard Henry Dana was the first American to travel along the California coast and write about it. In his 1840 memoir, *Two Years Before the Mast*, he was a young New Englander when he signed on as a merchant seaman for a two-year sea voyage from Boston to California and back. His ship stopped in ports along the coast during the period when *Alta California* was still a province of Mexico. In January of 1835, his ship landed in Santa Barbara.

"In the middle of this crescent, directly opposite the anchoring ground," he writes, "lie the missions and town of Santa Barbara, on a low plain, but little above the level of the sea, covered with grass, though entirely without trees, and surrounded on three side by an amphitheater of mountains, which slant off to the distance of fifteen or twenty miles. The mission stands a little back of the town, and is a large building, or rather collection of buildings, in the center of which is a high tower, with a belfry of five bells. The whole, being plastered, makes quite a show at a distance, and is the mark by which vessels come to anchor. The town lies a little nearer to the beach…and is comprised of one-story houses built of sun-baked clay, or adobe, some of them whitewashed, with red tiles on the roofs. I should judge there were about a hundred of them; and in the midst of them stands the presidio."

After a diet of deprivation and wild weather around the Cape of Good Hope, Dana and his fellow seamen were thrilled to discover during their journey along the coast of central California that fresh beef was not only plentiful but "it was

cheaper here than the salt" — a testament to the number of ranches producing beef, and the limited markets for the meat. Dana also provides fascinating commentary on the local peoples' dress, ranking, predilection for finery, and beautiful speaking voices. ("A common bullock driver, on horseback, delivering a message, seemed to speak like an ambassador at a royal dance.")

What surprised him the most during his trips ashore in Santa Barbara and Monterey Bay was the amount of silver being passed around. "I never, in my life, saw so much silver at one time, as during the week that we were at Monterey. The truth is, they have no credit system, no banks, and no way of investing money but in cattle. Besides silver, they have no circulating medium but hides, which the sailors call 'California banknotes'. Everything that they buy they must pay for by one or the other of these means. The hides they bring down dried and doubled, in clumsy oxcarts, or upon mules' backs, and the money they carry tied up in a handkerchief, fifty or a hundred dollars and half dollars."

Dana also observed the settlers' extraordinary horsemanship skills. "Horses are as abundant here as dogs and chickens were in Juan Fernández. There are no stables to keep them in, but they are allowed to run wild and graze wherever they please, being branded, and having long leather ropes, called lassos, attached to their necks and dragging along behind them, by which they can be easily taken. The men usually catch one in the morning, throw a saddle and bridle upon him, and use him for the day, and let him go at night, catching another the next day. When they go on long journeys, they ride one horse down, and catch another, throw the saddle and bridle upon him, and, after riding him down, take a third, and so on to the end of the journey. There are probably no better riders in the world." [This and previous quotes are all from *Two Years Before the Mast*, mentioned above.]

It is understandable that skilled horsemanship was mandatory and horses were plentiful. The distances were vast, the populations were cut off from cities, the terrain and weather were conducive to easy breeding, and wealth was measured largely in livestock.

With the rush of gold prospectors to California after 1849, the ranchos experienced a period of prosperity, for suddenly there was a rapidly growing market for meat, as opposed to just hides and tallow. Life on the ranchos, however, didn't change much over the following decades, revolving as ever

around the land, the seasons, and religious and social gatherings like fandangos (dances), weddings, baptisms, barbecues, brandings, and saint days. Gambling was also popular, particularly the Mexican/Spanish card game Monte, which resulted in huge debts, often satisfied with livestock or land.

H.T. Liliencrantz offers a glimpse into the rancho lifestyle in his memoir, *Recollections of a California Cattleman*. The author had spent time in his youth on his family's ranch in Aptos, near Santa Cruz, where he had become close to the family of Don Vicente Castro. Castro was the father of seven children and the son of the owner of a Mexican land grant ranch, Aptos Rancho, but his father had by then sold off most of the ranch. When the Castro family decided to move south, buying some acreage of Rancho Tepesquet east of Santa Maria and adjacent to Rancho Sisquoc, Don Vicente was asked by his friend, John T. Porter of Watsonville, who in 1892 had purchased the Sisquoc with his associate, Thomas B. Bishop of San Francisco, to become *mayordomo* of the Sisquoc Ranch.

After a couple of years of receiving repeated invitations by letter urging him to visit the ranch, in 1900 Liliencrantz persuaded his father to allow him to make the entire roundtrip —approximately four hundred and twenty-five miles — alone on horseback. He rode for six days to reach Sisquoc and spent two weeks on the ranch before making the trip back.

His descriptions of life on Rancho Sisquoc are colorful and detailed. He describes a herd of 100 Angora goats, guarded by trained dogs all day when out at pasture; the rapid acquisition of cattle — 100 head here, 100 head there — from nearby ranches; and many, many horses kept for various uses (saddle, driving, and draft), as well as stallions and mares for breeding.

And he meets one of the first homesteaders in the Sisquoc watershed:

"One day a man appeared at the Sisquoc, the like of whom I had read about, but never seen; one of a pioneer sort, a combination of stockman, hunter, and trapper, a good looking fellow, in age something over fifty. He was garbed in fringed buckskin and was well mounted. He made a mid-day meal with us at the ranch house, and appeared to be well acquainted with Don Vincente. The conversation was entirely in Spanish. After he left the boys told me that his name was Goodchild and that he lived on the far eastern edge of the Sisquoc, having a homestead there in the rough mountains. He was English by birth, well educated, and had come to California as a youth, but had chosen for some reason unknown to them the rough life of a mountaineer rather than association with men of his kind and breeding. With a young Indian woman he made a home in the wilds and there they raised a family of half a dozen children, and made their living by hunting and trapping and raising a few cattle."

When the mountain man passed through again with a small band of cattle he was taking to market, he brought along two of his sons. "And then," says Liliencrantz, "I saw more buckskin apparel than I have ever seen except on Indians at the Frontier Days Show at Cheyenne…All three men carried six-guns, which was natural enough, their buckskin garments home tanned, cut and sewn. Altogether they were a picturesque lot."

The image of the Wild West was firmly imprinted on the author's mind when he pointed his horse north for the journey home. And as the century turned, so the ranchero era gave way to more modern times.

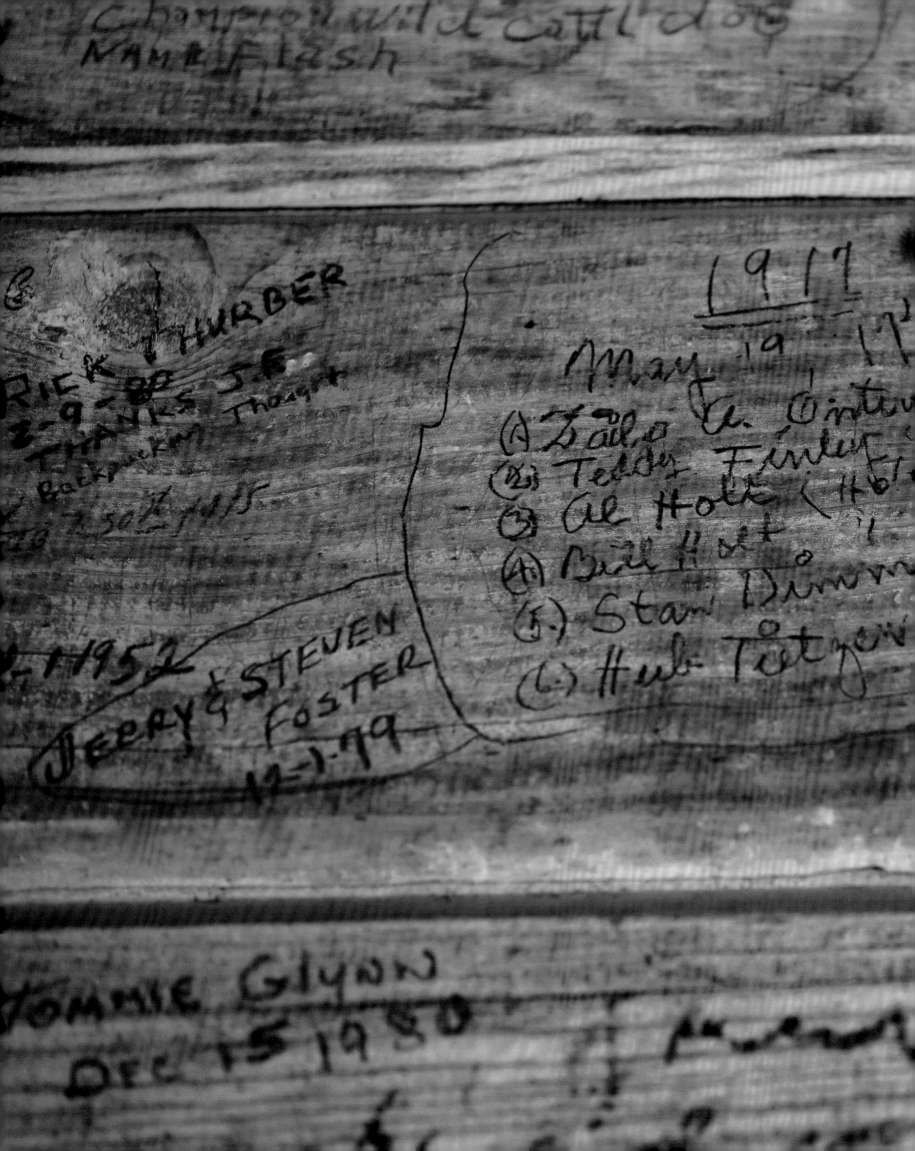

The New California

During the Spanish and Mexican rule of Alta California, the most desirable land — that which was accessible and had the best grazing and water rights — was apportioned through the land grants. In 1862, the American Government passed the Homestead Act, which allowed a person to acquire 160 acres as long as they built a structure and lived and farmed on the land for five years.

The western migration started by the Gold Rush was accelerated by the Homestead Act and it didn't take settlers long to find their way to the Santa Maria area. There was a twenty-mile stretch of available government land on the upper portion of the Sisquoc River from the eastern, or upriver, boundary of the Rancho Sisquoc grant. The only wagon access to it, however, was by road through the ranch and along the river, which included about thirty river crossings. Despite its inaccessibility, a community developed there of approximately a dozen families. By the late 1800s, there were around 200 people on about 20 homesteads in the area. They even had a schoolhouse, built in 1895, and a sawmill.

The settlers "all had their little orchards and their cows," explains Rancho Sisquoc co-owner Judy Flood Wilbur. "They were totally self-sufficient, but life expectancy was low due to disease, infections and the risk of childbirth." They grew vegetables, raised livestock, cultivated fruit orchards (apple, peach, and plum), and tended bees. One settler even made wine from his own grapes. In addition, there was ample fish and game. The homesteaders were known to make the three-day trip to Santa Maria to trade only a couple of times a year. In winters with heavy rains, they were sometimes cut off from contact with the outside world for two or three months at a time.

The homesteads were simple structures of logs or board-and-batten with rough-hewn floors, stone fireplaces and wood-burning stoves. An exception was the two-story Tunnell House, which William Tunnell built of pine lumber with sycamore tongue-and-groove flooring. The house was later used as a line cabin by Rancho Sisquoc and still stands today. With its recordings of fish catches, dates, and initials inscribed on its walls, some dating back to 1908, it is as much a piece of living history as it is a picnic destination.

One of the more charismatic characters in the settlement was Hiram Preserved Wheet, who arrived with his family from the Midwest. He practiced faith healing through the laying-on of hands and mandated strict dietary rules among his family and followers. (It's hard to believe, given the circumstances, but according to Robert E. Easton's account at the 1962 Pioneer Picnic, published in the *Santa Maria Times*, Wheet eschewed tobacco, liquor, animal fats, and milk, and only used coconut oil for cooking.) Wheet headed a group of about a dozen families, most related through marriage. He also ran the post

office — for only four months. It has long been rumored that the government officials shut it down when they discovered that Wheet could neither read nor write.

Jack 3 Finger Flat, an area along LaBrea, was named by Ralph Goodchild after a notorious pirate named Three Fingered Jack. A member of Joachim Murieta's Gang, Jack supposedly came ashore in Avila, found his way to LaBrea Canyon, and stayed for a time in an encampment of black tents. It has long been rumored that he buried treasure there. Many have attempted to find it, though no one has succeeded.

In May of 1895, an account written by a visitor to the settlement, published in the *Santa Maria Times*, described his trip: "Passing the Sisquoc ranch house, kept by the genial majordomo, Mr. Castro, about ten a.m. I arrived at my point of destination a little after twelve. This part of the road is very rough and rocky in places. The scenery of the deep canyon like valley is rugged and beautiful. Along the north hill slopes, the hills are yet as green as they were here in March. The south slopes, though, are drying."

Homesteading became increasingly difficult on the marginal land as problems with water, floods, and drought recurred. Rancho Sisquoc Cattle Manager Ron Davis grew up on Sisquoc homesteader lore. His great-grandfather and grandfather both homesteaded in the upper Sisquoc and his family ran the sawmill that produced all the lumber for the community, including the schoolhouse and the Tunnell House. "When my dad and his two brothers were about age ten and living on Manzana they'd go to school at Zaca Lake. They'd go on Mondays and come back on Fridays. It was a several-mile hike up Sulpher Springs Canyon and down to Zaca Lake. They were tough kids."

In 1896, according to the *Santa Maria Times*, there were 75 people present for the 4th of July. "Dance was again resumed in the evening and continued until midnight when a large bonfire was built around which a crowd gathered and feasted and sang songs until daylight. A few fireworks were set off in the evening and Ed Forrester in attempting to find out where the balls of fire came from, nearly got his whiskers burned off. It was a jolly crowd and a good time was had by all."

Over the following decades, however, the settlers started to drift away, some letting their land revert back to the government. By 1903 the school had only one student left. Of all the original homestead structures, the only ones still standing are the Tunnell House and the Manzana Schoolhouse (now a historical landmark). Beyond that, the only signs of the once thriving community of self-reliant individuals are the remnants of chimney stacks and some lonely gravesites.

Taming the Land

By the turn of the century, the Santa Barbara area had become inundated with Anglo-American migration. Selling property to the Americans was an attractive business opportunity and in 1899, Porter and Bishop formed the Sisquoc Investment Company (their holdings now extended beyond just the one rancho).

The Chumash had made use of the tar and asphalt they found in the Santa Barbara region, even using it to seal their canoes; the newcomers would find new uses. Mining began in 1850, with William F. Crocker of San Francisco leasing the asphalt and other mineral rights of Rancho Sisquoc. By 1897, the Asphalt Mine, located in the Zaca area in the southeast part of the ranch and worked by the Alcatraz Asphalt Mining Company, was sending liquified asphaltum by pipeline thirty-five miles west to Goleta for shipping. There were 120 men involved in the mine's construction; they and their families were supported with twenty buildings, a post office, a company store, and a schoolhouse on the remote site. According to Cattle Manager Ron Davis, they even had a baseball team.

After four years, when the operation was no longer profitable, the mine closed, with Crocker still holding the mineral rights. The land was later sold.

Robert E. Easton had studied surveying and engineering at U.C. Berkeley, graduating in 1898. When Thomas Bishop and John Porter bought Rancho Sisquoc, Easton not only knew Bishop's sons from college but his sister married Porter's only son. Easton was recruited to Rancho Sisquoc in the summer of 1899 to supervise a survey of the ranch boundaries.

"The only map back then was the old hand-drawn *desenio* from 1883," says Easton's granddaughter Joan Easton Lentz in her book, *Story of a Santa Barbara Birder*. "That was the original land grant and it showed property corners illustrated by rock formations or a massive oak tree, just pen-and-ink sketches.

"The ranch headquarters — located at the western edge of the property where the pasturelands were wide — held the barns, tack room, and a bunkhouse," she writes. "But up the Sisquoc River, back toward the eastern ridges, that's where the bulk of the land lay in the shape of a large rectangle. And if you rode most of the day on horseback, you would at last come to the border with the national forest. Then you hit the public lands. But in this hardscrabble country with no regulation, it might as well have been one big chunk, whether you were a homesteader further upriver or a Chumash Native American who came and went along the secret pathways."

In January of 1900, at the age of 24, Easton became the superintendent-manager of Rancho Sisquoc. Porter died in February and Castro, the *majordomo*, stayed on to assist until 1903, when Easton took full control. As Easton's son relates in his memoir, *Life and Work,* "He lived on the ranch for seven years as superintendent, de facto at first, later in full title, talking over from a fine Spanish gentleman named Vicente Castro, of the Castro family from Castroville. Vicente was a Spanish-Mexican-Californian of the old school. He knew cattle; he knew animals; he was pleasant, easy-going, and a wonderful gentleman. I remember him well, with a beard like God Almighty."

By this time access to the homesteads had been restricted; from 1899 the gate at the Rancho Sisquoc wagon road was kept locked, though the remaining homesteaders were provided keys.

Then, during his survey, Easton found a copper spike in an oak tree and recognized it as a marker. This brought the boundary of the ranch a quarter-mile farther north than previously recognized, overlapping some homesteaded lands along the upper Sisquoc River. Sisquoc Ranch bought out homesteaders George, Henry, and William Tunnell; Edward and William Forrester; H. P. Wells; Adolph Willmann; and Edward and Josiah Montgomery for $5 to $10 per acre. This plus a later purchase added an additional 2,200 acres. In 1930, Easton further expanded the ranch by buying 2,705 acres of the Holt Ranch, which was part of the old adjoining Rancho Tinaquaic, located in Foxen Canyon. (Foxen had had eleven children; after his death the land was split into eleven parcels. Rancho Sisquoc ultimately purchased three of those parcels.)

Between 1908 and 1910, new construction included the main house, guesthouse, and other headquarters buildings, including the barn, granary, shop, and sheds adequate for a massive operation, which in its heyday pastured between 2,000 and 3,000 head of cattle a year. In subsequent years, livestock numbers have fluctuated under the direction of various cattle managers, including Bill Walters, Roy Hardin, Dick Mays, Bill Caldera, Bob Schwarzkopf, Bob Hadley and Jack Ford. In 1910, Easton supervised the building of a $100,000 dam and pipeline on the Sisquoc River a few miles north of ranch headquarters. It was a major engineering accomplishment of the time, garnering press coverage in papers throughout Southern California. On November 12th, 1910, the *Santa Maria Times* reported, "The project is one of the largest engineering feats of the kind ever attempted in this part of the state and requires unusual precaution as well as good judgement. Mr. Livingston [the engineer] had to go down 38 feet to bed rock requiring an immense amount of excavation as well as a thorough pumping system to keep out the river flow." The purpose of the dam was not to store water, but to divert it through a pipeline to irrigate crops. At first it was successful, but drought and silt caused it to be abandoned around 1920. Years later it was repurposed and reconfigured as part of the modern irrigation system, which today provides water to the vineyard reservoir. Remnants of the system still exist today and can be seen around the ranch.

ASPHALTEA/"SISQUOC MINES" AND SCHOOL

ASPHALTEA/"SISQUOC MINES"
NOTE CABLE CAR SYSTEM WITH DOUBLE TRACK PASSING AREA

In 1910, one of the region's major feats of engineering took place on the Sisquoc River, at a location where the river disappears underground. Then Manager Robert Easton oversaw the building of a $100,000 dam and pipeline, a massive feat that garnered headlines in the newspapers throughout California.

In *Life and Work*, by Robert Olney Easton (with David Russell), Easton's son writes about growing up on Rancho Sisquoc. He describes Albert Romo, a significant ranch figure who taught him to ride when he was four. Romo was "a masterful teamster [who] could drive 6 or 8 horses with only reins attached to the leaders. He could also drive 6–8 horses with reins to each." A bachelor, Romo lived on ranch working six days a week for $30 a month, room and board included.

The most dashing figure on the ranch was Guadalupe Mendoza, whose father had been homesteader and was a leatherworker who specialized in making reatas and reins. Guadalupe "was still of an age to go away to parties on Sunday, and drink wine, and dance with girls. He would always go horseback. None of these people drove a car." He was a legendary figure to the young Easton, as he usually won the roping events in the local rodeo, as well as the annual prize from the local sporting goods store for first deer killed of the season. "Guadalupe was the head vaquero and he rode the most beautiful horses …," writes Easton. He was one of those who could rope and tie a wild steer along and if you don't think that's a job, try it sometime. To run down, and lasso, and throw and tie a thousand-pound or heavier wild steer or bull — which weighs more than you and your horse combined — try that sometime. He could do that." To top it all off, Guadalupe had charisma. "He wore a big sombrero and always wore chaps when he rode, a gray work shirt and gray trousers."

In the early days, the ranch used trained steers, or "cabestros" (Spanish for oxen) for various jobs recruiting brute force. "They had rings in each horn," recalls Easton. "They had big, wide-spreading horns with holes bored in them for iron rings and they were very tame. Only two were left when Father first came to the ranch. The vaqueros would take them back with them into the wild cattle range; and when they caught a wild one, they would tie him to the horn of the cabestro…who weighed maybe twelve hundred pounds, maybe as much as eighteen hundred, in any event much more than the wild one. And the wild animal would fight and struggle, and the big old oxen would just start steadily trudging home, and finally take him back to the ranch. It might take a day, or two, or three, or four, but he'd finally get back to the ranch with this wild animal all calmed down."

Youngsters were assigned the most menial tasks: hoeing weeds, milking cows, cleaning stalls. There was a toughness that was valued, and a decided lack of coddling. "If you asked for or seemed to ask for any sympathy you got ridiculed," Easton writes. "The whole idea was, how tough are you? You could sense this among the men: This is tough work, these animals are tough; the land is tough; the world is tough. How tough are you? That was the tradition that you're brought up in."

In 1951, the Sisquoc Investment Company sold Rancho Sisquoc to Mr. & Mrs. Edwin L. Green of Los Angeles and Claude Arnold of San Luis Obispo. It was then purchased in 1952 by James Flood, who had owned another land grant ranch, Rancho Santa Margarita y Las Flores, part of which became Camp Pendleton. Flood's goal was to run a working cattle ranch.

Seven Decades of Stewardship

By far the longest period of ownership in Rancho Sisquoc's history has been under the Flood family. James Flood had previously owned Rancho Santa Margherita y Las Flores, a 200,000-acre working cattle ranch located in San Diego and Orange Counties, which his father had purchased in 1882.

In 1942, approximately 125,000 acres of that property was appropriated by the U.S. Government and developed as Camp Pendleton, the U.S. Marine Corps' west coast base. (The Marine Corps' Camp Pendleton T & O logo originated as a cattle brand.) By then Flood had cattle in his blood, and after years of searching in multiple states for the right property, in 1952 he purchased Rancho Sisquoc.

James Flood was actually not the first member of his family to visit Rancho Sisquoc. In 1934, Betty Flood, then Betty Dresser, was a member of a "moving house party" that started in Southern California. As Betty told the story, "Our third stop was at Rancho Sisquoc as a guest of Bob Easton whose father was the manager. We three girls were housed in the guesthouse. In those days I smoked, and to my horror, I discovered I had burned a hole in great-grandmother's prized quilt! The next morning I confessed my guilt to Mrs. Easton and asked for a needle and thread which she promptly gave me. The rest of our group all went for a ride and a picnic while I stayed home mending. Eighteen years later I returned as owner of the Ranch."

The Floods would set out to transform the ranch into what it is today. Initially a cattle and farming operation, over the ensuing years the ranch diversified its business through vineyards, vegetable farming, a winery, oil exploration, and gravel mining.

From 1952 until his death in 1990, James Flood oversaw the ranch operations with day-to-day management by Howard Hamilton (1952–1956), William Walter (1956–1963), Harold Pfeiffer (1963–1986), and Edward Holt (1986–2018). In 1979 Rancho Sisquoc was incorporated as the Flood Ranch Company, with James and Betty Flood and their four children, Jim, Judy, Elizabeth, and John, as the original shareholders. Upon James Flood's death in 1990, his son Jim Flood assumed the role of president. He managed ranch business and daily operations in conjunction with managers Ed and Mary Holt, with shareholder meetings held annually for almost 30 years. In 2018, Judy Flood Wilbur and Elizabeth Flood Stevenson bought out their two brothers. Today they are co-owners and manage the ranch in conjunction with General Manager Steve Fennell.

Throughout Harold Pfeiffer's 23 years of management under James Flood, much was undertaken to bring the ranch forward and to diversify. Pfeiffer's laconic style and dry wit is captured in a 1989 memoir he wrote about his years at Rancho Sisquoc:

"The first crops I planted were sugar beets. All the fields in front of the headquarters to the front gate were planted to sugar beets. We grew some enormous beets but they were very misshapen due to sugar beet nematode in the ground. The next year we planted sugar beets on the lower mesa. We had a pretty good crop but had a hard time getting a contractor to dig the beets because of the rocks. We finally got someone from Bakersfield to get the beets out, but he said he would never come back."

When there was major flooding in 1969, he recounts: "Big flood in February and March of 1969 covered part of the orchard. Sammy marooned for about two weeks. Jim Hall of PG&E offered to get him out by helicopter but Sammy would not leave saying all he needed was cigarettes and dog food."

The ranch, even in the 1960s and 1970s, was a place populated by memorable characters. A vineyard manager lived in a trailer with his wife and simply disappeared one night. Another, Roy Hardin, was a cattle foreman. "I don't think I have ever seen anyone who could ride like Roy," write Pfeiffer. "He just seemed to be part of the horse."

In the 1960s, the cookhouse was ruled by Mrs. Moreno, known as "Bush," relates Judy Flood Wilbur. "Breakfast was at 6 a.m. sharp, eaten in stony silence, then followed by the orders of the day issued by the manager. Bush spent the day enveloped in a cloud of white cigarette smoke, making comments out the window or preserving fruit and vegetables, which were stored in the storm cellar under the cookhouse."

Pfeiffer and Flood worked very closely together for more than two decades. Together they tried a number of ventures, including oats, alfalfa, and seed beans. They dry farmed 400 acres of garbanzos and 400 acres of barley. (When they obtained wilt-resistant seed from U.C. Davis, they lost the entire crop to wilt.) They switched from barley to a Mexican variety of wheat, which did better in the coastal climate. With the bigger yields, they built grain storage tanks, but their timing was off; shortly afterwards prices for wheat declined due to overproduction.

In 1968 they leased several fields to a big local producer who successfully planted and harvested carrots. The relationship lasted only one season, however, due to the flooding of those same fields the following winter. A three-acre orange grove planted in the early 1960s was expanded to 40 acres in 1964 and 1965; three acres of avocados were then added to the orange grove. Between cold temperatures (which they attempted to warm using wind machines and smudge pots), flooding, and market difficulties, this effort was also abandoned.

Perhaps the duo's best idea was to plant grapes. Test plots of Reisling, Chardonnay, and Cabernet Sauvignon were planted in 1968 and a nursery established in 1969. In 1972, the same year the reservoir was dug on the lower mesa, the first harvest took place, with the first vintages being fermented in plastic garbage cans. By 1977 they were producing two wines and about 500 cases. By 1989, it was seven wines and 4,000 cases. Today, Rancho Sisquoc makes up to 10,000 cases of many varietals, including Merlot, Chardonnay, Cabernet Sauvignon, Sauvignon Blanc, Riesling, and Sylvaner. Rancho Sisquoc also sells grapes to other wineries and nurtures a dynamic and engaged wine club of approximately 1,500 members.

James Flood met famed Western artist William Gollings at the Auchincloss estate on Long Island when he was visiting his aunt as a college student. Gollings must have been taken with the young man's colorful ranching past. He created this artwork and wrote a note to its owner on the back.

Rancho Sisquoc has been a cattle ranch since the days of the land grant. The Floods always intended to honor that history, despite the vagaries of the cattle market. The ranch was purchased without cattle, but wild cattle were prevalent throughout the back country. A group of cowboys hired to capture them used an old trick of leaving a freshly butchered hide draped over a brush to draw the cattle. Although this lured them out of the impenetrable brush, it took two years to get the last one out. By 1963 the ranch had 600 cows and 200 purchased Mexican steers. At the time, the barley and oat hay grown on the ranch was fed to Sisquoc cattle. At one point, according to Harold Pfeiffer, the herd numbered 1,200–1,500 and since then has settled somewhat below that, depending on conditions. Various brands have been throughout the ranch's history, starting with the original Sisquoc brand, an S inside a Q. An "F" brand (used on native Sisquoc cattle) was added later, along with a backwards F with backwards J, which was used on purchased cattle. Improvements in the 1990s included a new squeeze chute and updated corrals at the ranch headquarters; the original scales and slaughterhouse are still standing today.

A long line of cattle managers and cowboys — including Bob Swarzkopf, Bob Hadley, Jack Ford, Dick Mays, Roy Hardin, Bill Caldera, Bill Walters, Ken Windsor, George Beggs, Bill Rutherford, Porter Daniels and Doaney Nogues — include current Cattle Manager Ron Davis. Davis's roots on the Sisquoc River go back to his grandfather and great-grandfather, who homesteaded in the area. He has been responsible for Rancho Sisquoc cattle for more than three decades. Elizabeth Flood Stevenson, now a farmer in Idaho, credits Ron for helping form her own conservation ethos. "Ron has been there for 35 years, and his family lived up the river from our place during the homesteading period in the late 1800s," she says. "Ron is the cattle manager, but more importantly is the 'caretaker' of the ranch. He has taught me the importance of not interfering with nature. He protects all the wild animals in an endeavor to keep everything in balance. At every water trough, one can see a small ramp to allow the quail and small animals access to the water. His cattle grazing techniques are in harmony with the seasons. He has them trained to come when he calls to them. I never cease to learn from this true conservationist."

From top: Harold Pfeiffer, long-time Rancho Sisquoc manager who worked closely with James Flood; together they were among the first to plant grapes in Santa Barbara County. Elizabeth Flood Stevenson planting oranges. Jim Flood and Harold Pfeiffer at a ranch celebration.

Local knowledge, says John Flood, is crucial. "It was passed down in families; they learned from one generation to the next. They are really good land managers, in my mind. They'd graze one area then get them out. They also did controlled burning." According to John they also employed tactics like pushing the younger cattle into the high rough country to build muscle, and also putting them into areas known for ticks, which in older animals can cause health problems but which in younger animals builds immunity.

Ron Davis combined his years of observations on the ranch with the study of holistic range management through Stan Parsons Ranching for Profit School. "We don't want a herd of 'riparian huggers' that overgraze the easy pickings along the rivers," he told writer Steve Suther of the *Angus Beef Bulletin* in 2008. "So we select and train cattle to forage on the slopes." They also give heifers an extra year of growth and maturity before breeding them.

Ed Holt was hired by Harold Pfeiffer in 1977. Originally the vineyard manager, he became general manager in 1986. He and his wife, Mary, raised their four children on the ranch, with Sarah Holt, their youngest, becoming Rancho Sisquoc's winemaker, a position she held until 2019. Ed Holt planned the production facility at the winery, developed the McMurray Vineyard, and oversaw all aspects of the ranch. Mary Holt started working on the ranch full-time in 1988. As winery manager and bookkeeper, she did administrative work, worked with wine distributors, organized special events,

and managed sales for the winery and tasting room. She was particularly involved with the Rancho Sisquoc Wine Club, which was founded in 1988 and now has approximately 1,500 members (thirty of whom are original Charter Members and still actively participating today). She also worked closely with the Santa Barbara Vintners Festival, which has held its annual event at Rancho Sisquoc off and on for many years. In 2018, Ed and Mary retired, having worked for Rancho Sisquoc for 41 years and 30 years respectively.

In 1994, the ranch ceased its own farming operations and began a leasing agreement with Adam Brothers Farming to cultivate broccoli, cauliflower, peppers, tomatoes, and celery on approximately 45 acres. Over the years the acreage under vegetables has increased, and the partnership with Adam Brothers continues to this day.

In 1999, Betty Flood planted 256 olive trees running the length of the ranch driveway to the headquarters. Today the trees produce two kinds of exceptional olive oil, Manzanilla and Mission. The bottles sport labels bearing a whimsical line drawing done by Betty's granddaughter Brett Stevenson. The image of Betty standing on the porch of the Tunnell House wearing her cowboy hat and wooly chaps seems an apt representation of James' and Betty's style, as well as their vision for the ranch. It was one that combined adherence to tradition with the embracing of innovation and new ideas. It is a vision that still guides decisions today.

Three members of the Holt Family — Mary, Ed, and Sarah — were instrumental in the operation of the ranch for four decades: Ed as General Manager, Mary as bookkeeper and winery manager, and Sarah as winemaker.

Life on Rancho Sisquoc

Both Betty and James Flood were larger-than-life characters. Despite not living full time on the ranch, they were fully present in all decisions and present in actuality as much as possible. James Flood loved working with large machinery; when not needed in the office, corrals, fields, or vineyards, he could usually be found on a grader or tractor. One time he was grading a steep part of the road called the 101 between the Dam Corral and Crazy Springs. When he stood up to answer the call of nature, the tractor tilted, slipped, and started sliding down the steep incline. James rode the tractor all the way to the bottom, emerging with lots of bruises but no broken bones. After that, that stretch of road was called the "1-Uh-Oh."

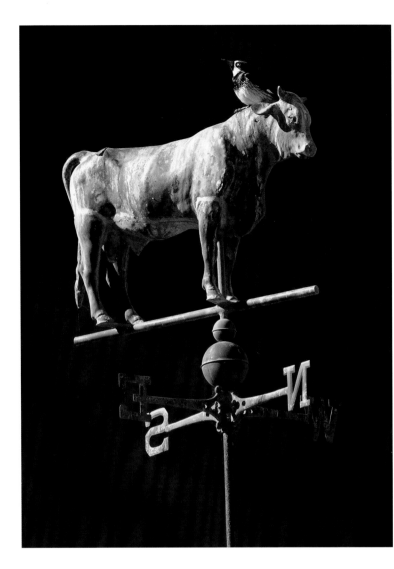

Road work was not only dangerous but extremely difficult in some of the more impenetrable and steep sections of the ranch — and there are 100 miles of roads on the ranch. "My father loved driving the graders and tractors," says John Flood. "He loved doing roadwork. He often got stuck and had to be pulled out. And when the roads got washed out, he loved it [because it meant he had to do more roadwork]."

Betty was equally charismatic, whether creating memorable Thanksgiving gatherings around the kitchen table in the original farmhouse, gathering watercress along the river, or helping gather cattle. Even in her 90s, Betty still insisted on driving wine club guests to the vineyards in the old 1956 Land Rover. "It was considered the highlight of the day for wine club members to drive out to the vineyard in the Land Rover with Mrs. Flood," says Judy Flood. "They loved it but we were terrified she'd go off the cliff. She was 93, driving a 1956 Land Rover with no brakes. I told her it was not really

prudent. She wrote, 'Join me at your own risk!' on a piece of paper and posted it on the windshield. She was so mad at me, she made seven trips that day." Eventually, family members took to removing the spark plugs from the vehicle so Betty couldn't start it.

Deanne Musolf Crouch, writing in the *Santa Barbara News-Press* recounts her experience of the wine club's Day at the Ranch in August of 1999. "Betty Flood, an incredibly handsome and fit 82-year-old woman in a crisp khaki blouse, trim jeans and cowboy hat, ushers us out to her jeep, top down. 'Step into my chariot,' Betty urges, and we climb aboard." Later, when discussing the ranch's cattle operation in a visit with Jim Flood, Crouch is told that Betty still rides out with the cowboys to help move cattle.

To celebrate Betty's 80th birthday, Judy and her children organized a three-day campout for thirty-two family members at the Tunnell House. Tents were erected and meals cooked on site each day by a caterer who drove up from town. Days were filled with games, skits, treasure hunts, hikes, horseback rides, and fun. Evenings were spent sitting around the campfire sharing memories under the night sky.

It is fitting that the family members would mark their mother's later years in such an adventurous, logistically complicated, and memorable way. The four Flood children — Jim, Judy, Elizabeth, and John — spent much of their childhoods traveling back and forth to the ranch, sometimes by train from San Jose to San Louis Obispo, where they'd eat club sandwiches in the dining car. "When our family dogs grew to six, we started driving," recalls Elizabeth. "My mother collected dogs; we had so many strays."

It was an unusual way to grow up, but for the Floods it was just what they did. They would spend a month or more on the ranch every summer, Judy recalls. "The big highlights of summer were getting up at 5 a.m. and having breakfast with the cowboys and Mrs. Moreno. She'd ring the bell on the main house. There would be five or six cowboys. In those days they ran cattle way up above Tunnell House. It was a 10- or 12-mile ride to Tunnell House; we'd camp there and look for cattle then go from there into Abel Canyon, Manzana, and other areas. We'd bring them back to Tunnell House where there were corrals, a water trough, the river, and a spring. We'd also round up in Media Portrero, a big area north of there. We spent a lot of time riding with the cowboys."

Elizabeth has similar memories. "A typical summer day began with breakfast in the original cookhouse with the employees," she says. "It consisted of gooey eggs, raw bacon, lots of coffee, and cigarette smoke. Conversation was limited to 'yep' and 'dunno.' Then we would catch the horses, saddle up, and head out to gather cattle. Pete, my favorite horse, had the SQ brand on his left cheek. My parents loved this activity, as did my younger brother, John. He and I would follow Doaney, an entertaining fellow who would show us his beer stash hidden in the creek. Often after riding on hot summer days, we headed to Bee Rock on the Sisquoc River. We kids fished, played in the swimming hole, and built forts. My father insisted that we eat the fish we caught, even though they tasted like river moss."

"Hollywood really made an impression on me, with the Sisquoc backing it up," recalls John Flood of his childhood. "I grew up with Mark Twain, Tom Sawyer, Roy Rogers, Gene Autry. I was the adventurous young rebel who just wanted to be outside. I romanticized cowboys; they were my heroes. When I was one, Father bought the ranch and I pretty much grew up there. Every summer, every Easter holiday, our family would drive down. We had a two-horse trailer with a big old Town Squire station wagon loaded with dogs, hamsters, chickens. We'd drive down Highway 101 and it took five and a half hours with frequent stops to feed all the animals."

When the Floods were children, the cowboy culture was still very much alive. The ranch buildings included the bunkhouse, cookhouse, shop, sheds where the wagons were stored, and three barns: two for hay and for feeding cattle and one for horses, with hay storage in the middle. "I remember my mother said that my father's mother, when she came and saw the ranch, said, 'You're going to clean this place up, right?' He said yes…but it took a long time."

For John, the allure of Rancho Sisquoc was strong and he spent five years living and working there as a young adult. Among ranch workers along the central coast, he says, "The desire to work at Sisquoc was very high. Every cowboy had four, five, sometimes six horses each. Their corral horse was a reining horse who could work cattle in small spaces and in the open." This was essential since the cattle "didn't see people that often. They were so wild they would hide in the sagebrush. The cowboys would lure them out with hay then push them down the valley to corrals where they could brand, castrate, and vaccinate." The corrals were tall and made of cables that were wrapped around stout oak trees to anchor them then woven with sagebrush. "They had to have corrals built like a fortress. If you had corrals like today's they would have just jumped out of them, like deer."

The historic Tunnell House has been the venue for many a gathering, from family picnics to Betty Flood's three-day 80th birthday extravaganza. John Flood was strongly influenced by time spent on the ranch during his childhood; he worked there as a young adult and later became a major force on the competitive cutting-horse circuit.

Because the distances were so far, and because if one got stuck, injured, or unseated from a horse there was no way to summon help, a telephone line was eventually strung from headquarters to barns to corrals to Tunnell House — one wire for fourteen miles, according to John. "Each corral had a crank telephone and each had a battery and carried a low voltage current. You cranked it once or twice, long or short, kind of like Morse Code, and you answered depending on the ring."

John describes trips by horseback with the ranch cowboys and a few neighbors into the area that is now Los Padres National Forest. "We'd ride eight days with a cart full of steel posts, axes, shovels, food, water, and hay for the horses. We'd take 500 heifers and we'd go almost all the way back to Sisquoc Falls. It was very rough country and hard on the horses." For a ten-year-old, though, "it was a dream come true, living the cowboy life, under the stars."

It wasn't all work, however. Betty's sister Jean Law and her husband Ward were constant companions, and Judy remembers summer adventures with Joan (Law) Gamble and Peter Law, cousins who were as close as siblings. Everyone would fish and swim at Bee Rock, a wonderful swimming hole about seven miles upstream from the headquarters, go deer hunting, and shoot pigeon and quail up LaBrea and Long Canyons. As teenagers they all learned to drive the five-gear stick shift Land Rover.

"Then there were the endless exploratory Jeep rides, headed up by my father," Elizabeth adds. "Uncle Ward was always along entertaining us by putting bananas in his ear. He also had to saw down trees that had fallen across the road. The ranch was a child's paradise, from bottle feeding calves to rustic camping trips. There were the usual complaints from us about the 'work' we had to do, such as washing and drying the dishes by hand. My mother and Aunt Jean built all the rock walls by hand, on the terrace (with our help, of course), while my father and uncle directed the construction. The walls are still standing after 70 years."

Flood family memories include swimming at Bee Rock (Elizabeth Flood and John Flood); Betty's mother, Elizabeth Dresser, known as 'Ganno'; Jeep rides (Peter Law and Jim Flood in front, Judy Flood and Joan Law in rear); trail rides; and shooting (John Flood after a successful quail hunt). Children were allowed to pack a lunch and disappear for hours; Elizabeth would mount her horse Stormy and head for the hills.

This page: On a ranch it's best to
always have a shovel at the ready.
A wild raccoon lived with the family
for several months before heading
back into the wild. Opposite page:
The ranch kept a team of draft horses
into the 1990s. On one occasion,
Uncle Ward Law and Dick Hyde flew
down from the Bay Area and landed
on the Big Mesa. A shooting group.
One of John Flood's otters, Oscar,
enjoying a river outing.

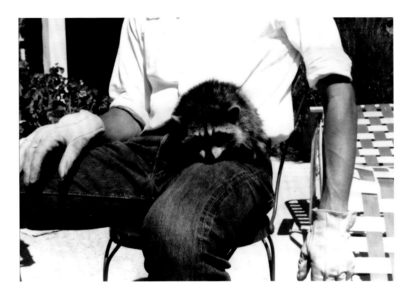

Wildlife was ubiquitous on the ranch: wild turkeys, wild boars, beavers, and rattlesnakes were frequently sighted. Skunks lived under the house. Bears were known to come to the MacMurray Vineyard to feast on the Merlot.

Hunting was a part of ranch life from the earliest days. When Judy Flood Wilbur and her siblings were growing up, she recalls, deer hunting was a common pastime for everyone, often with the cowboys.

"The slaughterhouse was used to skin and butcher the deer and most of the meat was made into jerky which the cowboys put in their saddlebags to eat when they were rounding up cattle." Quail are found throughout the length of the valley and are also frequently hunted.

"Hunting season with my older brother Jim was my favorite activity," recalls Elizabeth. "I would hang out in the slaughterhouse with my brother and his friends. I was given scraps of meat, from which I made sun-dried jerky. I learned the art of butchering from my brother."

"I can still pluck a bird in no time flat," Judy adds. "Jim would kill the birds and, as the little sister, I had to pluck them."

Fun was also a recurring theme for the Flood family at Rancho Sisquoc. They worked hard but they also played hard. From picnics and trips to the river's best swimming hole to zany skits and golf games and made-up entertainment for house guests and wine club members (such as Cow Chip Bingo), there was always time for fun between the hard work. John recalled that his sisters would sneak down to the barn and braid the horses' manes and tails when the cowboys were at lunch. One time while driving along the

river in the dusk, his older brother Jimmie told him to grab a gunny sack to catch some animals by the roadside. He couldn't see what it was beyond a dark shape but managed to catch them, at which point he heard snarling. "We got home, and our mother was cooking dinner. It turns out they were raccoons; he wanted them as pets. They escaped about three months later and went into the wilds." Years later, when he went to visit Judy, who was living in Thailand at the time with her husband, he bought Oscar, Jr. as a companion for his American river otter, Oscar. The two otters lived in a room in the Woodside house and would travel in the car to the ranch to visit, ride in the Rover, and swim in the river. "I'd take them on a walk every day. They were either passed out, feet in the air, or going 100 miles an hour. My dad said they were a cross between a cat and a monkey, and it was true."

Guests were frequent, including Aunt Jean Law, Betty's sister, and Tinki Somers who was adept at butchering game. On one occasion, Uncle Ward Law and Dick Hyde flew themselves to the ranch and landed on the Big Mesa. The family always had about five dogs, Elizabeth raised robins she found in the barn, and riding was a way of life, both western and English, in Woodside and at the ranch.

"My mother always had her own horse and they all could rope but if you asked them to do a sliding stop or you tried to collect them they couldn't do that; they just walked out," says Elizabeth. "My father loved donkeys and mules and teams of horses; he had a team of beautiful gentle sorrel work horses. He loved buying all these animals. Some worked out, some didn't."

Even though they were young, they weren't coddled. "No one ever waited on us," says Judy. "We had to do everything ourselves." The Floods believed kids on a ranch had better be self-reliant. They learned to drive early and practiced driving stick shift on the old Land Rover. John remembers one day assembling pipes in a pasture where a heifer seemed to be having trouble calving. He was told to drive back to the shop to get help. "I couldn't reach the pedals and I had only driven a few times. I was twelve at most. Somehow I got back and got help." When he arrived back at the pasture he was shown how to help a cow birth. "It was my first experience pulling a calf." He laughs. "It's not the way I'd do it today."

The kids were allowed to take lunch and ride out alone. And they were taught how to find their way home if they didn't have a horse to guide them, Judy explains. "Daddy would take us out. He'd say, 'If you get lost just follow the water downstream.' Then he'd leave us. It was a long walk home."

When Betty wasn't moving cattle or building rock walls, she did the cooking and laundry. James spent his days outside in the vineyards, on horseback, and working alongside the men. He'd take guests and his children on hours-long Jeep rides explaining every aspect of the land, the cattle, his newly graded road, and the vineyards

"What I saw," says Elizabeth, "was them working together. I was four when they got the place. It was just a dirt pile. It was a working ranch. They didn't concentrate on lawns and trees, but they spent a lot of time cleaning it up and fixing it up. They did everything themselves. They built the rock walls; they went out and picked up the rocks. A lot of the time it was my mother doing the work and my father directing," she laughs. "My mother did all the gardening. There was no architect, no interior designer. Their goal was to have it be a ranch, not to turn it into a showplace. My parents didn't want to change anything. They kept it a ranch and it still is a ranch. It's still authentic and that's what makes it different from other places."

When James Flood died in 1990, son Jim assumed responsibilities for management of the ranch, alongside managers Ed and Mary Holt. Under Jim's tenure over three decades, ranch infrastructure was modernized, vineyards were expanded, and wine sales were increased. Working with Steve Will of Coast Rock, James embarked on major works that mitigated flooding and reclaimed lost farmland. He also got a new road constructed on the north side of the river to allow year-round access to the vineyards and vegetable fields there. At the same time, he focused on cattle sales and farming operations, helping modernize and streamline those efforts. The Wine Club was launched under Jim's watch, with Mary Holt taking the active lead. This helped the winery grow and achieve more consistent sales. It also created a strong sense of community. Under Jim's management and his nurturing of the relationship with Rancho Sisquoc's distributor, Joseph Franzia's Classic Wines, the winery expanded dramatically, with production varying year by year from a few cases at the beginning to 20,000 at the height, and approximating more than 10,000 cases a year today.

Clockwise from top: Jim Flood ran Rancho Sisquoc for three decades after James Flood's death. James Flood at the McMurray oil drilling site in 1980. Betty Flood and others out on the land. Longtime Cattle Manager Ron Davis working cattle in the corrals.

General Manager Steve Fennell came to Rancho Sisquoc with a background in wines rather than ranching; he says he has learned much in his time at Sisquoc. "I look at it as a thrilling challenge in which all areas can be the focus," he says. "The diversity of the ranch and the history of the ranch makes it unique. The family has a history of ownership and commitment to keeping it in the family and keeping it viable and vibrant. I take it very seriously and try to keep it moving in the right direction, not to just maintain it but to improve as much as possible. I see my role as keeping the operation successful and moving it forward but maintaining the family's ethos and supporting all the people here. It's been very rewarding," he adds.

In the 1960s, James and Betty Flood were featured on the cover of *Fortune Magazine*. In the photo they stand on the cliffs above ranch headquarters, thoroughly in their element, the Santa Maria Valley falling away behind them as the river makes it way to the ocean. From the same spot looking east the ranch feels limitless, with layers of hills and mountains receding in the distance as one's eye extends toward the wilderness in the Los Padres National Forest. The couple did their best to honor the land, instill respect for it in their children and grandchildren, and maintain its history and legacy while still making it viable in the 21st century. The next generation has every intention of doing the same.

Clockwise from top left: James Flood on the cliffs above the ranch headquarters. Ranch Manager Steve Fennell discusses ranch business with Cattle Manager Ron Davis. The recently installed solar array makes the ranch more energy efficient.

Vineyard
View

Fifty years ago, Rancho Sisquoc owner James Flood and his ranch manager Harold Pfeiffer made the decision to plant grape vines on ranch property. It was a bold move; they were among the very first to plant grapes in the Santa Barbara area. But Flood had noticed that the area's climate and soil compared favorably with the renowned growing regions of Napa and Sonoma.

"My understanding in reading Harold Pfeiffer's report and hearing the stories growing up," says James' eldest daughter, Judy Flood Wilbur, "was that Harold was told to always feel free to try different crops to see what might work. When the orange grove failed because of frost and the rising costs of labor, Harold suggested that Daddy plant grapes. As a result we were the first, or one of the first, in the Valley to plant grapes. Daddy [later] helped Steve Miller, the owner of Bien Nacido Vineyards in Santa Maria Valley with his first vineyard."

The move proved fortuitous, explains Matthew Dennis Kettman in *Vines & Vision: The Winemakers of Santa Barbara County*. "The glories of growing wine grapes in the Santa Maria Valley are well documented: With a wide mouth opening onto the cool Pacific, it stays quite cool in all seasons, with huge diurnal shifts in temperature, allowing grapes to ripen over a long season while retaining acidity. Rancho Sisquoc enjoys similar qualities, but because it is so far up the valley, it also gets more warm sunshine."

In 1968, Harold Pfeiffer and James Flood decided to plant test plots of Reisling, Chardonnay, and Cabernet Sauvignon vines, the success of which led them to plant 100 acres of vines. They started a nursery in 1969 then planted 29 acres in 1970, 48 acres in 1971 and 28 acres in 1972. In 1974, 87 acres were planted, followed by 18 more in 1981. The first Rancho Sisquoc wines were bottled in 1972 under the private reserve label of James Flood with the "F" Brand on the label. Five years later, the winery was bonded and the first commercial wines released under the Rancho Sisquoc label. Harold Pfeiffer crushed the first Cabernet Sauvignon, using only estate-grown grapes, with a baseball bat and trash can. In 1977, he recalled in his notes, "We had three dairy tanks and a wooden tank for fermenting. We also had one small press and a hand corker." In the early years, wines produced were Cabernet, Riesling, and Rosé of Cabernet and Pfeiffer had a funny story about the Rosé. "In 1980, David Champion was wine maker. He let the Rosé of Cabernet go completely dry. In desperation, we blended some Johannesburg Riesling into it to add a little sweetness. We won our first gold medal with this wine." Other winemakers included Stephan Bedford, who for more than a decade was instrumental in raising the profile of Sisquoc wines in the early years; he is now proprietor of Bedford Winery.

By the 1990s, approximately 10,000 acres throughout Santa Barbara County had been planted with grapes. The vintners were just starting to understand the unique characteristics of the region, shaped largely by the fact that the valleys here run east to west rather than north to south, in contrast to the rest of the west coast. Since the initial planting in the late 1960s of nine acres of Johannesburg Reisling and forty acres of Cabernet Sauvignon, Rancho Sisquoc Winery now has more than 300 acres under cultivation in two vineyards, the 200-acre Flood Vineyard, planted in 1999, and the 100-acre McMurray Vineyard, planted in 2000. A new production facility was built in 1994 while several buildings have since been added for wine production and sales. These support the production of anywhere from 10,000 to 20,000 cases per year. While the Santa Maria Valley is known for Pinot Noir and Chardonnay, the Sisquoc vineyards bottle varieties like Sylvaner (produced in only one other California vineyard), and all five varieties of Bordeaux.

Sarah Holt Mullins was raised on Ranch Sisquoc. Her father, Ed Holt, worked at the ranch for 41 years. He was made vineyard manager in 1987 then served as overall manager of the ranch for 32 years, until 2018. In 2014 Sarah became Rancho Sisquoc's winemaker. When interviewed for Kettmann's book *Vines & Vision: The Winemakers of Santa Barbara County,* she said, "I'm trying to make wine that showcases this ranch. We're tucked way back out there and I just want to bring our wines to the forefront."

In 2019, Sarah Holt moved to Ohio, at which time the assistant winemaker, Steve ("Smitty") Smith — who grew up nearby and had been at the ranch since 2008 — became head winemaker.

Other longtime winery staff included Francisco (Juan) Gutierrez, who was hired on to Rancho Sisquoc as an irrigator in 1976. He originally came to California from Mexico and taught himself English by watching television. By 1978 Juan was working in the vineyard and in 1986 he was named vineyard foreman, a position he held until his retirement in 2017.

The Rancho Sisquoc winery is busy year round, hosting drop-in visitors, tour groups, 'Sisquoc Saturdays', and large festivals. The friendly cat, Jezebel, is a ubiquitous presence around the Tasting Room. For 25 years, siblings Jim and Judy Flood poured wine together at the annual Day at the Ranch for Rancho Sisquoc Wine Club members. Opposite: Winemaker Steve "Smitty" Smith; longtime Vineyard Manager Francisco "Juan" Guiterrez; Tasting Room Manager Becki Rodriguez with her dog, Pete.

Rancho Sisquoc sells most of its grapes to other producers, but saves 40 acres' worth of the most special fruit for its sixteen varieties of wines, many of which regularly receive scores of 88–91 points by *Wine Enthusiast* and *Wine Spectator*. Sisquoc's estate wines have won multiple awards at various events, including the 2016 California State Fair, where they took home a gold and four silvers. More recently, the 2016 Pinot Noir and Syrah both received gold medals and scored 92 points in the 2019 Sunset International Wine Competition. In the 2020 San Francisco Chronicle Wine Competition, Sisquoc wines were awarded Best of Class for the 2017 Cabernet Franc, Double Gold for 2017 Cabernet Sauvignon, plus an additional three golds, four silvers, and two bronze medals.

In keeping with its multi-generation, one-with-the-community ethos, the Rancho Sisquoc winery has created a welcoming tasting room and relaxing picnic area with tables, shade, and expansive lawns. Visitors who drive out for the day can pick up a bottle of wine and some nibbles; they are welcome to bring a picnic and relax for as long as they like. Birthdays, reunions, and other events are often celebrated there, with many returning year after year.

Over the decades, Rancho Sisquoc has built quite a following around its wines. There's an active and loyal wine club for whose members the perfect weekend involves a visit to Rancho Sisquoc. The club was the brainchild of Mary Holt and Jim Flood. Launched in 1997/1998, it now consists of approximately 1,500 members who receive complimentary tastings, generous discounts, and invitations to special events. During Sisquoc's annual Day at the Ranch event, some 350-plus members attend the private gathering at the Ranch to celebrate their special relationship with the winery. In the early days they would ride in the old Army truck or with Mrs. Flood in the Land Rover, crossing the river several times to get to the Flood Vineyard and then return to the headquarters for an old-style Santa Maria barbecue done in the pig pot barbecue. As time went on and the membership increased, they were driven to the McMurray Vineyard in air-conditioned buses or rode with Mrs. Flood. At the vineyard, they tasted wine under a tent and planted their own vines, which they numbered and could then check on each year to monitor progress. Upon returning to the ranch headquarters, they enjoyed Santa Maria barbecue, music, and different games each year. One of Jim Flood's favorites was Cow Chip Bingo. After all the bets were placed, a cow would be let into a corral marked off with squares to see where she would leave her mark.

Many of the wine club's 30-plus active charter members still regularly attend Sisquoc's Day at the Ranch (although it had to be cancelled in 2020 and 2021 due to the pandemic). And over the years, Tasting Room Manager Becki Rodriguez has had ample opportunity to get to know them. "The charter members have become friends; one charter member even gave a kidney to another," she says. "It's very much a family."

The highlight of the annual Day at the Ranch party for Rancho Sisquoc Wine Club members was being driven out to the vineyards by Betty Flood in the old Army truck, which lacked brakes. In her later years, Betty further delighted members by posting a hand-made sign saying, "Ride at Your Own Risk".

Charter members Howard and Trudy Smith live in Ventura County, within easy distance of Rancho Sisquoc. They love the wines — "they're consistently good, year after year," says Howard — as well as the ambience of a working ranch. "It's a nice drive up the coast to the winery and once there it's so quiet and serene." For them, says Trudy, the Day at the Ranch is one of the year's highlights. "I don't think we've missed one." The Smiths recall being driven out to the vineyards by the elegant Mrs. Flood, and they fondly remember the year they got to plant their own vine, which they numbered so they could check on its growth and compete in good-natured contests with the other members year after year to see whose vine had produced the most grape clusters. The Smiths have been Sisquoc regulars long enough that they remember when the olive trees were planted along the drive. "And now they're selling the olive oil," says Howard.

Astrid McLean and her husband had been tasting wines in the Los Olivos/Santa Maria area since the 1980s; they became charter members of the Rancho Sisquoc wine club in 1997. "They were the first to offer a wine club," Astrid recalls. They enjoy the whole Sisquoc experience. "We love the wines, the location is beautiful, and we really like the people," she says. "I like that they grow grapes that are not available anywhere else, like Sylvaner and Malbec; it's hard not to be pleased with the selection, and the wines are reasonably priced. The Day at the Ranch is always fun — especially when Betty was still driving the old Army truck!" The McLeans joined the club when their children were little; now the eldest is of age to taste wines too.

Sisquoc is one of 16 stops along the Foxen Canyon Wine Trail, a 30-mile route from Los Olivos to Santa Maria. The wine trail brings day trippers from Los Angeles, Santa Barbara, and Monterey as well as international tourists. In addition to the Wine Club's annual Day at the Ranch, held in the summer, Rancho Sisquoc hosts the Santa Barbara Vintners Festival. In the early years the event was held twice a year, with the hosting responsibility shared with Firestone Vineyard. "They would host in the spring, we would host in the fall," recalls Judy Wilbur. "We were the only wineries that could handle that many people." Over the years, the Santa Barbara Vintner's Festival has been through various iterations, often attracting as many as 2,000 wine enthusiasts to Rancho Sisquoc.

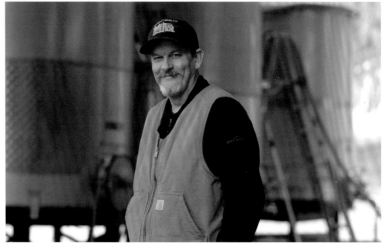

General Manager Steve Fennell
out in the vineyard; enologist,
cellerman and photographer
Steve McCrank in the winery.

The ranch's expanse of outdoor space proved a boon during the pandemic, providing a place of solace and enjoyment for the house bound. The tasting room is open for pickups every weekday and for pickups, purchases, and tastings on weekends. In the summer, the ranch hosts Sisquoc Saturdays, with live music and food trucks. It is evident that casual visitors enjoy the experience of visiting a historic working ranch on their winery tour. Yelp reviews are overwhelmingly positive — both for the wines and the experience. The most common refrain seems to be: "Out of the way, but entirely worth it." Everyone notes the relaxed, unpretentious, dog-friendly vibe, (and, of course, the affectionate, oversized winery cat, Jezebel). "If you are looking for a relaxing and rustic view," says one reviewer, "this is definitely the place for you! We drove out to the ranch at about 11 a.m. and it was so peaceful. The cows were roaming, the cats were napping on property, and there was even a sweet dog that greeted us." Another local reviewer wrote, "I want to live here. Please. I'll work for wine. Haven't joined a wine club in years but this place just speaks to us. Great wine. Great people. Great spot."

Steve Fennell, the current general manager of Rancho Sisquoc, grew up under the influence of his grandfather, who crossbred grapevines as a hobby. After summer jobs working in agricultural research for Heinz, he studied oenology at U.C. Davis. He has been a winemaker since the early 1990s, in Napa, in Australia, and at the Sanford Winery in the Santa Rita Hills. He feels blessed to be producing wine in Santa Barbara County, challenged by farming under increasingly dry conditions and a warming climate, and lucky to manage a 37,000-acre ranch whose wine business is just one aspect of the overall picture. "I look at it as a thrilling challenge," he says. "The diversity of the ranch and the history of the ranch makes it unique. I take it very seriously and try to keep it moving in the right direction, not to just maintain it but to improve it as much as possible."

In the introduction to *Vines & Vision,* Kettmann writes, "Santa Barbara is the most dynamic wine country in the world right now, a geographically blessed landscape full of diverse wine styles, stunning vistas, and personalities powered by natural curiosity and fierce independence."

Clearly, James Flood and Harold Pfeiffer were two of those curious and independent personalities. With their visionary planting of rootstock fifty years ago and the production of award-winning estate wines today, Rancho Sisquoc has earned its accolades — as well as its unique position within the Santa Barbara wine community.

Culture & Community

It's first light on an early spring morning at Rancho Sisquoc. The air feels wet and heavy but the rain holds, as it has for much of the rainy season. While there are no spring blooms on the steep grassy hillsides (this won't be a superbloom year), the land is a vibrant green. Cowboys are unloading horses from an assortment of trailers clustered around the old Pole Barn and tacking up their mounts. They move at the sure pace of people who know exactly what they're doing: without hurrying and with no unnecessary steps.

After a last sip of coffee, they mount up and head as one up the road, past the horse barn and the old Aermotor windmill, then into one of the pastures on the valley floor where they'll start gathering cows and calves ahead of a long morning of branding.

In some ways life at Rancho Sisquoc endures as it always has, linked as it is to the seasons and the weather. Calves are born, calves are branded, steers are sorted; vegetables are picked, grapes are harvested. Life moves at a steady pace throughout the year. The branding today will be done the old way, by a group of friends, relatives, and neighbors who have come together to gather cattle from the pastures, health check, doctor and sort the animals, then rope and brand the calves. Afterwards everyone will enjoy an old-style Santa Maria barbecue, a local tradition that dates back to the time of the vaqueros.

Rancho Sisquoc has always maintained a cattle operation. Originally used for grazing cattle and some sheep, the ranch has diversified its activities into farming, wine, and some mining, but it has never lost sight of tradition. In 1881 there were 660 head of cattle, 4,200 sheep, and 19 horses who were maintained on ranch grasses and oats. During Robert Easton's 50-year tenure as manager, the focus shifted to cattle, between 2,000 and 3,000 head a year. Depending on weather and the market, the ranch has always been a cow/calf and "stocker" operation. Today the number of animals varies from 600 to 1,000 head, with approximately 15–20 horses to move them between pastures and round them up for medical check ups, branding, and sale. The new way of moving cattle using ATVs is not for Rancho Sisquoc. And according to Cattle Manager Ron Davis, herding dogs "can ruin your day." As for horses, he says, "You couldn't do it without them."

As the cowboys push the herd through a lane lined with sycamores to the corrals at headquarters, the sun rises, the air warms, and jackets come off as the sorting and then the roping begins. Throughout the morning the camaraderie and close-knit relationship between the men — and the shared history between the men and the ranch — is evident.

Ron Davis grew up on and near the Sisquoc and has worked on the ranch for four decades. Ron's family relocated from Kansas to homestead upriver from the ranch; his great-great-grandmother is buried in the backcountry, just a rock wall marking her grave. Luke Hardin is the ranch farrier, and son of former Rancho Sisquoc Cattle Manager Roy Hardin. Brian Billington is the vendor of cattle supplements to the ranch. Tyke Minetti never misses a Rancho Sisquoc branding — and in fact had helped brand 150 calves the previous day at a nearby ranch on the Pacific Ocean. A ranch neighbor and longtime friend of cattle managers Ron and Chris, Tyke brought along his son Tommy and Tyke's longtime ranch hand, Chino. Tyke's great-nephew Wayne is also present. Williams's great-grandfather was Raymond Cornelius, who is pictured in the famous black-and-white photograph of old-time cowboys with their dogs in front of the ranch's Tunnell House after a day of rounding up wild cattle in the backcountry.

Chris Jorge's uncle, Manuel Jorge, who came to the U.S. from the Azores at age 12, is a competitive team roper whose skill helps make the work go quickly. Chris's wife's uncle, Greg Mier, was a member of the branding crew, as was another relative, Jim Gracia, a sixth-generation Californian who was Chris's father's partner in a cattle business.

The assistant ranch manager of Huasna Land and Cattle, Ty Gonsalves, lent a hand, as did another friend, Tim McDonald, who helps with brandings along the central coast area. The crew was rounded out by Cheyne Torres, a former co-worker of Chris's, and Rancho Sisquoc employees Jesus Vargas (whose father also worked at the ranch), and Antonio Salazar.

The annual gathering and branding brings together a group of people with historic ties to the ranch for a day of cattle work followed by a traditional Santa Maria barbecue. Assistant Cattle Manager Chris Jorge, right, is one in a long line of cattle managers and cowboys to work at Rancho Sisquoc.

As the animals move through the gate into the corrals, two men focus on counting. As they file past, Ron Davis observes, "They're smaller and lighter this year, on account of the lack of rainfall." As the work proceeds over the course of the next few hours, the men work in quiet rhythm. The last animal is a small white-faced calf who evades capture for a time before being "headed" by Williams and "heeled" by Manuel Jorge. A few minutes later — and five hours after the work began — Jorge and his horse stand catching their breath as everyone else heads to the gate to dismount and put away equipment. Chris Jorge approaches Manuel, pats his horse on the neck and says, "Good work, Uncle." The cattle work completed, the group moves to the horse barn, a historic wooden structure still partially filled with hay bales. Tables with red-checked tablecloths have been set up and a grill — laden with meat cooking over red coals and bathing in smoke from the native red oak — is positioned just inside the door. A feast of salads, beans, bread, and fruit is laid out and as the meat comes off the grill everyone grabs a plate and finds a place at the tables.

Joining the cowboys for the meal are a number of other friends and family members including Assistant Cattle Manager Chris Jorge's wife, daughter, and baby boy, and Jorge's wife's aunt, whose husband Greg lent his roping skills to the morning activities. "My wife and her aunt Sharon did the cooking of the beans, salad, and desserts," says Chris Jorge; "they are both excellent cooks. The meat was choice tri-tips with Santa Maria-style seasoning. The wood is red oak and was cut here on the ranch. The lunch was served in the Horse Barn, where all the ranch and working horses were stabled in the old days and is still used to store horse tack and saddles today."

The barbecue is a time-honored tradition at any branding that takes place along California's Central Coast region. It is fitting that for a *New York Times* article titled "In Search of the California Barbecue Tradition," writer Tejal Rao started his journey just west of Sisquoc in Santa Maria. He describes how the barbecue tradition in central California dates to the time of the vaqueros, who used large skewers to roast their meat over open fires of native red oak. Over the generations, some of the particulars have changed (prime rib versus tri tip, for instance) but the essence, and the sides — local pinquito beans (a regional specialty that's a cross between a pink bean and a small white bean), and garlic bread or grilled bread dipped in butter — have remained the same. From cattle work to barbecue, a Rancho Sisquoc branding is a celebration of tradition, culture, community, and a tribute to the generosity of the land.

The town of Sisquoc lies off the beaten path. Not much more than a hamlet, it is still considered remote today. Life there is centered on agricultural pursuits, and its people are brought together through family ties, work, the land, holidays, and church.

The San Ramon Chapel is the town's primary local landmark. It stands on a small bluff overlooking the entrance to Rancho Sisquoc and serves as a symbol for the town as well as for the rancho; (its distinctive silhouette adorns Sisquoc's wine labels.) The church owes its style to that of the California Missions that predated it and was built by local leaders in memory of Benjamin Foxen, one of the first American settlers in the valley. Located at the entrance to Rancho Sisquoc and Foxen Canyon, the property on which the church and cemetery were built was purchased by Frederick and Ramona (Foxen) Wickenden from the U.S. Government sometime in the 1870s then donated as the site for the church.

"On a hilly prominence, stands the Chapel of San Ramon, built in 1875 by the Wickenden family," writes John R. Wickenden in *From Rancho Tinaquaic and the Chapel of San Ramon*. "The year 1875 was a very dry year with almost no grass in Santa Barbara County. Frederick Wickenden drove his sheep north in search of feed and found grass in the Salinas Valley. Driving them on to Redwood City, he sold them for one dollar each. With the money, he purchased redwood lumber at the mills and arranged for it to be shipped to Port Harford, near the town of Avila Beach. The lumber was loaded into wagons and "teamed" to the ranch. There was the lumber to build the church so desperately needed by the community. Inspired by Reverend McNally of the Mission Santa Ynez, Frederick Wickenden, Thomas Foxen, and Chris Lawson are thought to have done most of the work themselves. Once completed, it was consecrated as the Chapel of San Ramon. Benjamin Foxen's body was moved to the new church's cemetery where one can see Foxen's tombstone, a marble shaft meant to replicate the broken mast of a ship."

The chapel was officially dedicated in 1879, when Bishop Francis Mora gave it the name San Ramon in honor of Saint Raymond Nonnatus, the patron saint of agriculture and farming. In 1966 the Benjamin Foxen Memorial Chapel became the first historical landmark in Santa Barbara County. In 1975, the renamed San Ramon Chapel was dedicated as California State Historical Landmark #877. Upon the 100th anniversary of the chapel, on August 31, 1975, mass was celebrated by Father Bartin Foxen; since then weekly services have been held every Sunday. In 1998, Lisa Flood and Thomas Dewell were married in the San Ramon Chapel with their dog, Moose, attending them as Best Dog. They were driven from the church by a team of ranch draft horses pulling a vintage Rancho Sisquoc wagon and delivered to their wedding reception, held in the Bull Barn.

With Foxen, Wickenden, Ontiveros, and others representing the valley's original settlers, San Ramon Chapel is place where time stands still, where past and present merge.

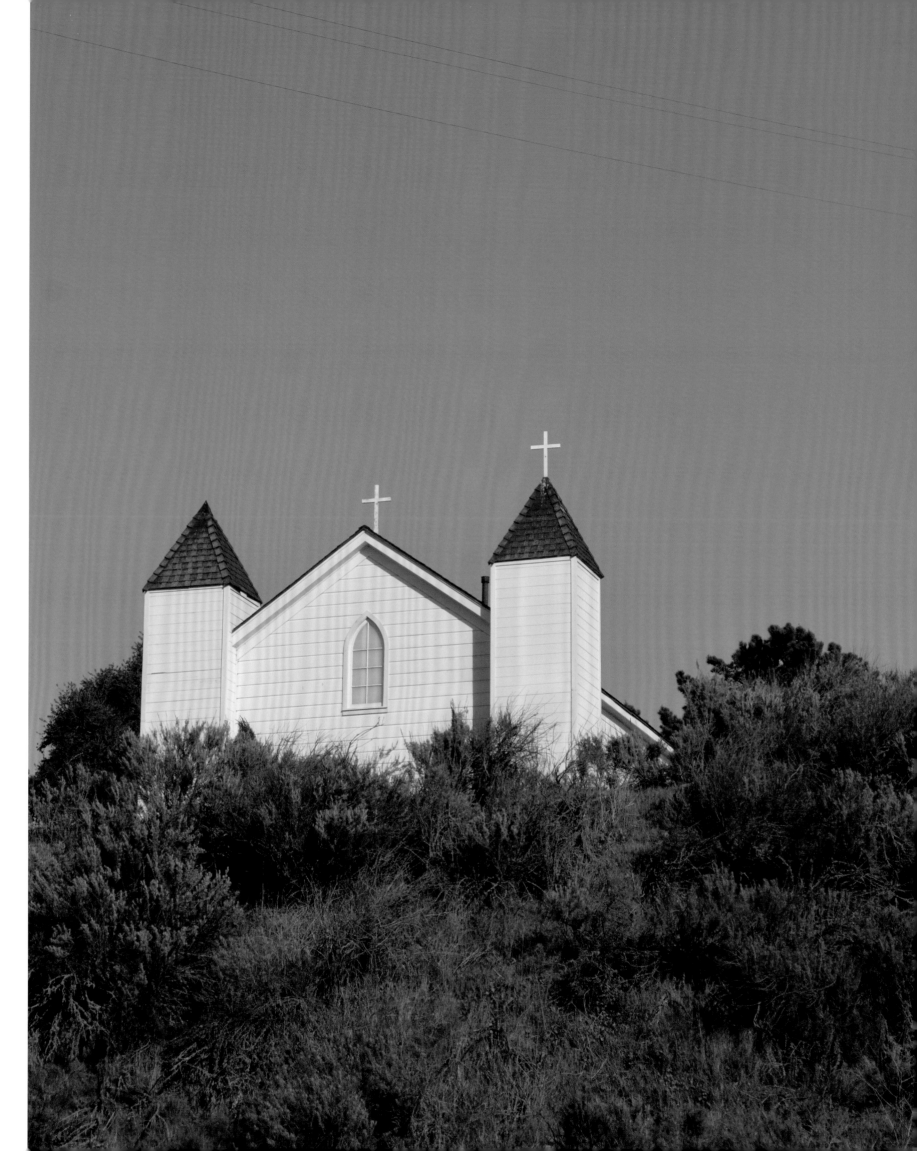

Inspired By The Land

Whether it's the light and atmospheric conditions or its great expanses of landscape, California has long had a strong art tradition, attracting established artists as well as tempting the untrained to pick up a paintbrush.

At the turn of the 19th century, European-trained plein air painters flocked to Southern California. They were attracted to Los Angeles and its environs by the region's magical quality of light and its wide array of subject matter, from desert landscape and beach scenes to rolling hills and snow-capped mountains. Sisquoc Ranch, encompassing a vast river drainage and extending through a variety of terrains into completely untamed forest lands, has proven an inspiration to artists for generations, its expressions ranging from crudely documented catches on the walls of Tunnell House and amateur watercolors from the early 20th century to beautifully realized oil paintings by recognized artists.

While there are said to be cave art drawings hidden undisturbed in the far reaches of what is now designated national forest, the earliest known artistic efforts on ranch property take the form of watercolors painted on Sisquoc Ranch by Cecil Wray Goodchild, a sixth-generation Californian born in 1901. A self-taught artist, he became known for his oils, watercolors, pencil sketches, wood engravings, and serigraphs. Although he spent most of his life in San Louis Obispo and Los Alamos, his roots on Sisquoc Ranch went deep. He was descended from James Goodchild, one of the earliest Sisquoc area settlers, who homesteaded in the far reaches of LaBrea Canyon. Goodchild's works capture an earlier, rougher time of simple utilitarian structures — such as the 1899 Tunnell House and the Manzana Schoolhouse — honestly rendered. It is fitting that he also painted the mission-inspired architecture of the San Ramon Chapel; Goodchild's gravesite lies in the Foxen Cemetery beside the chapel.

San Ramon Chapel; watercolor by
Cecil Wray Goodchild.

Ellen Easton too has deep roots on Sisquoc Ranch, and her experience growing up under its influence also inspired a career in art. A Santa Barbara native, her childhood was informed by her grandfather's and father's relationship to the ranch. Her grandfather had managed the ranch for 50 years, her father had grown up there, and Ellen was raised with a deep appreciation for California's wild places. When during high school she spent time in the art studio of a friend's father, two passions merged. She went on to establish the Easton Gallery in Montecito and got involved with a group of plein air painters called The Oak Group. Over 28 years she fostered a community of artists celebrating the wonders of California's landscape.

"This area has had an art movement since the 1920s, with the establishment of the Santa Barbara School for the Arts, which had artists like Ed Borein on its teaching staff," she says. "Early painters were drawn to the region because of the unique beauty of the mountains, the oceans, the light, the seasons. People fell in love with it, literally, and wanted to capture the spirit, light, colors, and shapes that make up our unique landscape."

As she worked with her own group of artists, all focused on the landscape, she reveled in curating "a group of people who could capture what I'd experienced out on the land." Inspired by a lifelong fascination with early California history and the land grant era, in the 1990s Easton conceived of a book project that would document the region's history ranchos. *Ranchos: Santa Barbara Land Grant Ranchos* was published by the Easton Gallery in 1996.

"Both my grandfather's and my father's life had been tied to the Sisquoc Ranch," Easton writes in the foreword. "I had grown up listening to the exciting stories and adventures of ranch history. My father, who loves and knows this land intimately, often took my sisters and me into the back-country. These early horseback and camping excursions were a wonderful schooling in nature: names of mountains, rivers, watersheds, which trail led where. We shared the thrills of seeing condors soaring overhead, exploring caves filled with Indian drawings, fishing for trout for our dinner, and sleeping out under the stars."

It was this deeply felt experience as a child that fostered her interest in art — particularly that of the central coast and the still wild interior ranch lands and national forests — and ultimately inspired the Ranchos Project. The task was to document each land grant ranch from the Mexican era, pairing artist to ranch to best capture the special characteristics of each property.

Ray Strong had a storied art career, having helped found the Art Students League of San Francisco, where he studied and taught with such luminaries as Maynard Dixon; he also painted murals for the Works Project Administration during the Depression. Strong's oil painting "Sisquoc Ranch" captures the prospect from the riverbed looking east into the mountains. The elongated dimensions help convey the magnitude of the river valley as it opens toward the town of Sisquoc and flows east toward the ocean. His palette ranges from yellow in the dry riverbed, green in the vineyards, and burnt umber in the foothills to purple on the west-facing mountainsides. In contrast, a more intimate work painted on nearby Foxen Canyon Road employs softer colors befitting a bucolic scene of redwing blackbirds alighting from rushes along the roadside with golden-toned pasture and hills beyond. "Ray saw beauty everywhere," comments Easton. "He's always been fascinated by erosion and the energy of the land and he loved the wild, wide open spaces there. His paintings are a celebration of the landscape."

Tunnell House; watercolor by
Cecil Wray Goodchild.

Sisquoc Ranch, by Ray Strong.

Watercolors by Cecil Wray
Goodchild. *Rancho Sisquoc,* oil
painting by Meredith Abbott.

Meredith Abbott, a graduate of Art Center in Los Angeles, has been practicing her craft for five decades. She also painted on Sisquoc for the *Ranchos* book. "Meredith Abbott is one of the premier landscape painters in Santa Barbara right now," says Easton. "She's extremely talented and was up for anything, early morning or late, and would go all day. At Sisquoc, I just showed her the ranch and she chose the subject that resonated with her." Abbott's work is serene. It captures the view across a green horse pasture to an iconic barn that appears almost white against the line of trees that mark the river. Beyond, the hills rise precipitously, with a phalanx of rugged mountains rising to the east under a gentle sky. The work captures the dramatic contrast of the tamed lands of the ranch headquarters against the untamed wilderness beyond.

The project — both the book and the resulting art exhibition — was a resounding success, says Easton. "People really got behind it; it had never been done before. I'd call a ranch owner and ask if I could bring artists to paint and they invariably said yes. I just loved it and the artists did too. They got to go places they'd never been and between the land, the buildings, and the people it was just a really rich experience. It all ties into my love of Sisquoc Ranch through my father and grandfather. My father shared it with us and I shared it with my artists. It's a neat connection to the landscape and the artists here."

In more recent years, Jim Caldwell paid a visit to the ranch after having heard about it for years. Caldwell was trained at the Ecole des Beaux Arts in Paris and holds a master's degree in architecture from Yale University. Today he is both an architect and a prolific painter in the San Francisco Bay Area, as well as a teacher of painting and drawing at Filoli in Woodside. Caldwell's formative years were spent in California, in Woodside, where he'd grown up, and at the Cate School, outside Santa Barbara, where he'd attended high school with Jim Flood in the 1950s.

"Cate is on top of a mesa overlooking Santa Barbara and the Channel Islands, so I developed an early love for the landscape of the Santa Barbara mountains," he recalls. "My junior dorm room had a spectacular view of the sun setting over the ocean." It is only natural that he would be curious about the ranch his high school roommate grew up visiting and later ran for so many years. His 2011 visit to Rancho Sisquoc proved inspirational, resulting in a number of landscape paintings, from large works capturing the scale of the rolling hills to more intimate views of wooded hillsides. He was particularly taken with a group of cows that blocked the road for a time; he painted whimsical portraits of them in a placid, relaxed state. From San Ramon Chapel to Tunnell House, and from vegetable fields to vineyards, as he shot photographs to later pore over in his studio, he developed an appreciation for the vastness of the Sisquoc valley.

"I had no idea of the scope and variety of beautiful landscapes that awaited me," Caldwell says. "Sisquoc Ranch, and all of its diversity, embodies so much of what we think of when we imagine a perfect California landscape: ranch land with black angus cattle, vineyards, rows of tilled vegetables, gravelly river beds, steep golden hills with specimen oaks and thick shady evergreen forests. What more could a painter want?"

Rancho Sisquoc has always inspired creative people. As the sheer power of its grandeur remains undimishined, it will surely continue to do so. Robert Olney Easton grew up on the ranch, attended Harvard and Stanford, traveled the world, and became a gifted and prolific writer. In his oral history, *Life and Work*, Olney said, "The Sisquoc Rancho, at the head of the Santa Maria valley, is one of the most beautiful spots in all California."

Today, Rancho Sisquoc remains unchanged in its essence from its earliest days as a land grant ranchero. The world may have changed, with technology having extended to the remote corners of the planet, and procedures and means of livelihood, even on the ranch, having evolved. But Rancho Sisquoc's natural beauty, and its wildness, remains undiminished, its owners determined to preserve and keep it intact. It is for future generations to experience its sense of history and timelessness in a place that celebrates the past while looking to the future.

These pages and preceding:
Paintings by Jim Caldwell.

Timeline for Rancho Sisquoc
and the Santa Barbara Region

—	Region inhabited by Native Chumash people
1542	Juan Rodríguez Cabrillo arrives leading the first European expedition to the region
1769	Portola Overland Expedition
1775	Anza Overland Expedition (includes ancestor of Pío Pico)
1782–1786	Santa Barbara Pueblo and Mission established
1821	Mexico separates from Spain
1835	Richard Henry Dana arrives in Santa Barbara; later authors *Two Years Before the Mast*
1845	Rancho Sisquoc Land Grant of 35,400 acres granted by Governor Pío Pico to Maria Antonia Domínguez de Caballero [RS]
1846–1848	Mexican-American War; California becomes part of the United States; Treaty of Guadalupe Hidalgo provides that land grants would be honored
1848–9	Gold discovered in California
1851	Sisquoc Rancho sold to James B. Huie, San Francisco auctioneer, for $12,500 [RS]
1862	U.S. passes Homestead Act
1866	U.S. patents grant for Rancho Sisquoc to James Huie et al.
1874	Town of Santa Maria established
1875	San Ramon Chapel built
1880s	Sisquoc Rancho acquired by Rockwell Stone, San Francisco hardware store owner, after death of James Huie [RS]
1880s	Homesteading era begins on Upper Sisquoc River
1892	John T. Porter and Thomas Bishop acquirer Rancho Sisquoc; [RS] Vicente Castro, becomes *mayordomo* [M]
1892	H. T. Liliencrantz rides 170 miles each way to visit Vicente Castro and his family at Sisquoc Rancho; later writes the memoir *Recollections of a California Cattleman*
1895	Manzana School opens on Upper Sisquoc River
1898	Beginnings of Los Padres National Forest (under earlier name)
1899	Porter & Bishop form Sisquoc Investment Company
1900–1950	Rancho Sisquoc managed by Ranch Manager Robert Easton [M]

1903	Manzana School closes, marking end of homesteader era
1910–1912	Dam built on Sisquoc River in major engineering feat
1937	Sisquoc Condor Sanctuary established near headwaters of the Sisquoc River in Los Padres National Forest
1951	Sisquoc Ranch (now 41,300 acres) bought by Mr. and Mrs. Edwin L. Green of Los Angeles and Claude Arnold of San Louis Obispo [RS]
1952	Rancho Sisquoc purchased by James Flood to operate as cattle ranch. (In 1882, his father James Flood had purchased another land grant ranch, Rancho Santa Margarita y Las Floras, which was taken over by the government in 1942 to build Camp Pendleton. Santa Margarita had been partly owned by Pío Pico, who shared the land grant with Andrés Pico, but Pío Pico lost his share betting on a horse race.) [RS]
1952–1956	Rancho Sisquoc managed by Ranch Manager Howard Hamilton [M]
1956–1963	Rancho Sisquoc managed by Ranch Manager William Walter [M]
1970	Grapes planted on Bryan Mesa (Flood Vineyard)
1973	Winery built at Rancho Sisquoc headquarters
1979	Rancho Sisquoc incorporated into Flood Ranch Company
1986–2018	Rancho Sisquoc managed by Ranch Manager Edward Holt [M]
1988–2018	Mary Holt full-time winery manager and bookkeeper [M]
1994–present	Adam Brothers lease Rancho Siquoc lands for vegetable farming
2011	Jim Flood, Judy Flood Wilbur, Elizabeth Flood Stevenson and John Flood inherit Rancho Sisquoc following the death of their mother, Betty Flood [RS]
2018	Judith Flood Wilbur and Elizabeth Flood Stevenson purchase brothers' shares and become co-owners of Rancho Sisquoc [RS]
2019–present	Rancho Sisquoc managed by General Manager Steve Fennell [M]

[RS] RANCHO SISQUOC TIMELINE   [M] MANAGEMENT TIMELINE

Authors and Contributors

AUTHORS

JUDITH FLOOD WILBUR is co-owner of Rancho Sisquoc with her sister, Elizabeth Flood Stevenson, and is Chairman of the Board. She is also an owner of the Flood Building in San Francisco and serves as its Chairman. Judy has a long history of civic service. In 1976 San Francisco Mayor Moscone appointed her to the Asian Art Commission. She has since served on and chaired both the boards of the Asian Art Commission and the Asian Art Museum Foundation, during which time she co-chaired the $125 million campaign and ran two bond measures for the relocation of the Asian Art Museum from Golden Gate Park to San Francisco's Civic Center. Judy was elected to Hillsborough City School District in 1976; she subsequently served as board chair and founded the Hillsborough School Foundation. A former president and trustee of the Commonwealth Club and the recipient of numerous social service awards, she has served on many other boards, including Wilbur Ellis Company and the Asia Foundation. A graduate of U.C. Berkeley, she lives in Hillsborough, California.

CHASE REYNOLDS EWALD is the author of fourteen books on architecture, design, traditional craftsmanship, and the history and cuisine of the American West. A graduate of Yale University and the Graduate School of Journalism at U.C. Berkeley, she is a writer, editor, and consultant. Chase is the design columnist for *Big Sky Journal,* a senior editor of *Western Art & Architecture* Magazine, and a frequent contributor to *Cowgirl* and *Mountain Living* magazines. A former wrangler and backcountry cook, she also founded and ran a nonprofit educational guest ranch in Wyoming.

CONTRIBUTORS

EDMUND GERALD BROWN JR. served as California's Secretary of State and Attorney General, as well as mayor of Oakland. He was elected as the 34th and 39th governor of California, serving from 1975 to 1983 and 2011 to 2019. He lives on his family's historic property in Colusa County, California.

ELIZABETH CLAIR ("LISA") FLOOD is a writer and photographer. The author of six western design and lifestyle books, her articles have appeared in *Architectural Digest, Cowboys & Indians, House Beautiful, Elle Decor, Mountain Living,* and others. She lives in Wilson, Wyoming.

STEPHEN T. HEARST is vice president and general manager of Hearst's Western Properties. He is responsible for managing Hearst's extensive ranching, timber, and property operations, including the historic 83,000-acre ranch surrounding Hearst Castle and the 73,000-acre Jack Ranch in Paso Robles. He also manages commercial real estate holdings in the Bay Area, the Central Coast, and Los Angeles.

ERIC P. HVOLBOLL is a friend of the Flood family. His ancestors came from Mexico to Santa Barbara County in the 1700s where they have owned and operated ranches for many generations. A graduate of Stanford University (A.B. in History; B.S., M.S. in Applied Earth Science, and J.D.), he lives and farms on his family's historic La Paloma Ranch in Gaviota, California.

Land Grant Ranchos in Santa Barbara County

NAME	DATE	GRANTEE
Nuestra Señora del Refugio	1794	José Francisco Ortega
Rincon	1835	Teodoro Arellanes
Las Cruces	1837	Miguel Cordero
Jesús Maria	1837	Lucas Antonio Olivera & José A. Olivera
Suey	1837	Maria Ramona Carillo de Pacheco
Lompoc	1837	José Antonio Carrillo
Punta del Concepción	1837	Anatacio José Carrillo
San Julián	1837	José de la Guerra y Noriega
Tepusquet	1837	Tomas Olivera
Tinaquaic	1837	Victor Linares
La Zaca	1838	Antonio "Indigenous"
Los Álamos	1839	José Antonio Castillero
Santa Cruz Island	1839	Andrés Castillero
Santa Rosa	1839	*Francisco Cota*
Casmalia	1840	Antonio Olivera
Guadalupe	1840	Diego Olivera & Teodoro Arelianes
Cañada del Corral	1841	José Dolores Ortega
Todos Santos y San Antonio	1841	W. E. P. Hartnell
Dos Pueblos	1842	Nicolas A. Den
Cañada de los Pinos	1843	Seminary of Santa Ynez
Nojoqui	1843	Raimundo Carrillo
Cuyama	1843	José Maria Rojo
Las Positas y La Calera	1843	Narciso Fabregat & Thomas L. Robbins
Santa Rosa Island	1843	José Antonio Carrillo & Carlos Antonio Carrillo
Cañada de Salsipuedes	1844	Pedro Cordero
Laguna	1844	Luis Arelanes & E. M. Ortega
Lomas de la Purificación	1844	Augustin Janssens
Corral de Cuati	1845	Augustin Davila
Ex-Mission la Purissima	1845	Jonathan Temple
La Laguna	1845	Octaviano Gutierrez
Mission Vieja de la Purísima	1845	Joaquin Carrillo & José Antonio Carrillo
San Carlos de Jonata	1845	Joaquin Carrillo & Jose Maria Covarrubias
Santa Rita	1845	José Ramón Malo
Sisquoc	1845	Maria Domínguez de Caballero
Tequepis	1845	Joaquin Villa
Cuyama (2)	1846	Cesario Lataillade heirs
La Golita	1846	Daniel A. Hill
San Marcos	1846	Nicolas A. Den & Richard S. Den

Glossary and Place Names

Abel Canyon – named for homesteader

Alejandro – Spanish for "Alexander"; Alejandro Canyon was named for Alejandro Ontiveros, who had a hunting retreat nearby

Aliso/Alisal – Alder shrub or tree of the genus Alnus

Bee Rock and Canyon – Named for large rock where swimming hole was located

Branquinho Park – Named for mid-19th-century setters in the Santa Maria Valley

Bryant – Now called Flood Vineyard

Cachuma – Chumash word probably borrowed from a nearby village; means "sign"

Chivo – goat, canyon name

Cuyama – Chumash word meaning "clams," probably borrowed from an indigenous village nearby

Diseño – Spanish word meaning "design, draft, description or picture"; historically used to identify the original drawings of the California Land Grants

Figueroa – Spanish surname; José Figueroa was a governor of California in 1830s

Kelly Canyon – named after local person

LaBrea – Spanish for "the tar" or "pitch"

Manzana – Spanish for "apple," or "a (city) block of houses"

Manzanita – Spanish for "little apple," but actually a shrub common to the Western U.S. McMurray Vineyard

Monte — 19th century Mexican gambling card game

Montgomery Potrero – named for early homesteader

Potrero – Spanish for "pasture or paddock"; a potro is a colt or foal

Sisquoc – According to Gudde, a Chumash word meaning "quail." Also given to mean "meeting place"

Tejano Flat – "tejano" meaning a person from Texas

Tepusquet – An Aztec word borrowed by the Mexicans meaning "copper," or a coin of little value

Tinaquaic – Chumash word, no meaning known

Vaquero – Cowboy (from the Spanish word *vaca*, for cow)

Vurro Canyon – A surname, probably of Italian origin

Zaca – According to Hart, a Chumash word meaning "peaceful place"

Sources: Erwin G. Gudde's *California Place Names,* 1969;
James D. Hart's *A Companion to California,* 1978;
Spanish dictionary and local and online sources.

Acknowledgments

Any project of this scope, complexity, and beauty is the product of much collaborative work on the part of many people. *Rancho Sisquoc; The Enduring Legacy of an Historic Land Grant Ranch* is no exception.

This endeavor was inspired both by my parents, James and Betty Flood—who not only kept the property intact, but maintained its authenticity over many decades—and my children, nieces, and nephews and their children. It is for them that we strive to preserve the ranch.

This book would not have been possible without the gracious cooperation of my siblings, Elizabeth Flood Stevenson and John Flood, and their spouses. Our resident historian, Cattle Manager Ron Davis, along with Assistant Cattle Manager Chris Jorge, both have deep roots in the valley through their family histories and upbringings. They pulled together a remarkable community celebration in a traditional gathering and branding followed by a delicious Santa Maria-style barbecue for the benefit of the project.

Rancho Sisquoc General Manager Steve Fennell gave generously of his time as did the ranch's many friends in the area, including Ellen Easton, whose love for the land led her to pursue a career representing the region's landscape artists, and Eric Hvolboll, an attorney and historian who farms avocados and agave on his own family's historic land grant ranch.

The beautiful and personal remembrances penned by Stephen Hearst, Jerry Brown, and Lisa Flood add so much as forewords, each addressing a different aspect of the ranch's history. Joan Levy helped immeasurably with historic research, delving into place names and ownership timelines. We thank our publisher Gordon Goff, our editor Jake Anderson, and our talented designer, Pablo Mandel, who spent countless hours working with us in Zoom sessions from another continent. His calm, upbeat demeanor and keen eye for design made this undertaking a wonderful experience.

We were incredibly lucky to have a professional photographer among the winemaking staff. Steve McCrank's beautiful images capture the day-to-day and season-to-season glory of Rancho Sisquoc—the vineyards, wildlife, winemaking, farming, and spectacular scenery. We could not have done it without him.

A special thanks to my husband, Richard Otter for introducing me at a social occasion to his friends Charles Ewald and Chase Reynolds Ewald, and for Dick's support throughout this entire project. Finding a writer of Chase's experience amongst our friends was serendipitous. Her passion and enthusiasm for ranch life, animals, western history, and rugged landscapes was palpable throughout the year and a half we've worked together. Chase's background and writing style were perfect for this book, and it was a pleasure and great fun for me to have the opportunity to work with her.

The publication of *Rancho Sisquoc; The Enduring Legacy of an Historic Land Grant Ranch* marks my family's 70th anniversary as owners of Rancho Sisquoc and the 50th anniversary of our winery. The real impetus for this project was to honor my parents, James and Betty Flood, their descendants, and generations of general managers, cattle managers, ranch hands, and vineyard and winery workers who have worked so hard on behalf of Rancho Sisquoc.

This book pays tribute to a special place and the people who have lived on and loved that place. Together we strive to memorialize Rancho Sisquoc's storied history while carrying its traditions forward, embracing the future, and preserving the land for the next generation.

— Judy Flood Wilbur
with Chase Reynolds Ewald

ORO Editions
Publishers of Architecture, Art, and Design
Gordon Goff: Publisher

www.oroeditions.com
info@oroeditions.com

Published by ORO Editions

AUTHORS
Chase Reynolds Ewald and Judith F. Wilbur

FOREWORDS BY
Edmund Gerald Brown Jr., Stephen T. Hearst, and Eric P. Hvolboll

PROLOGUE BY
Elizabeth Clair Flood

PROJECT MANAGER
Jake Anderson

BOOK DESIGN
Pablo Mandel / circularstudio.com

Typeset in Minion Pro

10 9 8 7 6 5 4 3 2 1 FIRST EDITION

ISBN: 978-1-954081-24-6

Color Separations and Printing: ORO Group Inc.
Printed in China.

ORO Editions makes a continuous effort to minimize the overall carbon footprint of its publications. As
part of this goal, ORO Editions, in association with Global ReLeaf, arranges to plant trees to replace those
used in the manufacturing of the paper produced for its books. Global ReLeaf is an international campaign
run by American Forests, one of the world's oldest nonprofit conservation organizations. Global ReLeaf
is American Forests' education and action program that helps individuals, organizations, agencies, and
corporations improve the local and global environment by planting and caring for trees.

Photographs by Steve McCrank:
Cover image; Pages 2–3; Page 4 (chapel); Page 14; Page 20; Page 25; Page 28, top and bottom; upper left; Page
30; Page 31; Page 39, lower right; Pages 46–47; Page 48; Page 51, upper right; Page 52 top and bottom; Page 53;
Page 54; Page 55 lower left and lower right; Page 57; Page 58; Page 59; Page 60; Page 72; Page 93; Page 95; Page
97, all; Page 102, All; Page 103, lower left; Page 108, All; Page 111, Top and Bottom; Pages 112–113; Page 125,
Bottom; Page 126; Page 128; Page 129, Top and Bottom; Page 130 top and lower left; Page 132, Top; Page 133,
Upper Right; Page 134; Page 136, Lower Left; Page 137, Left; Page 138, Right and Left; Page 146, All; Page 148;
Page 149; Page 153; Pages 178–179.

Photographs by Chase Reynolds Ewald:
Half title page; Page 6; Page 8; Page 11; Pages 18–19; Page 22; Page 26; Page 27, upper left; Page 28; Pages
31–32; Pages 34–35; Pages 36–37; Page 42; Page 45; Page 50; Page 56; Page 61, top and bottom; Page 62; Page
63, upper left and bottom; Page 67; Page 69; Page 75; Page 77; Pages 78–79; Page 89; Pages 90–91; Pages
98–99; Page 101; Pages 104–105; Page 106; Page 109; Page 110; Page 118, right; Pages 120–121; Page 125, Right;
Page 139; Page 140; Page 142, All; Page 143; Pages 144–145; Page 147; Page 150; Page 151; Pages 168–169

Photograph by Lisa Flood, page 67